P9-CFQ-229

BAR AND BAT MITZVAH IN ISRAEL
THE ULTIMATE FAMILY SOURCEBOOK

Judith Isaacson
Deborah Rosenbloom

1998

Bar and Bat Mitzvah in Israel
The Ultimate Family Sourcebook
by Judith Isaacson and Deborah Rosenbloom

Israel Info-Access

©1998 by Judith Isaacson and Deborah Rosenbloom
All rights reserved. No part of this book may be reproduced or transmitted in any form or by any means, electronic or mechanical, including photocopying, recording or by any information storage and retrieval system without written permission from the authors, except for the inclusion of brief quotations in a review.

Library of Congress Catalog Card No. 97-76734.
ISBN 0-9660877-0-4.
Printed in the United States of America.

Cover photograph: Abohav Synagogue, Safed.
Cover design by Toby Klein, Fungo.

TO OUR CHILDREN
◇ MICHAL ◇ EITAN ◇ JOSH ◇ LILA ◇
WHO OFTEN SHOW US THE WAY.

To Rachel
Of Blessed Memory

Entries for this book are based solely on suitability. No organizations or commercial establishments paid for inclusion in the *Sourcebook*. Facts, telephone numbers, faxes and addresses have been checked carefully. Such details were included so you can be sure the establishment or organization is operational during the relevant dates. Every effort has been made to make the *Sourcebook* as complete and as accurate as possible.

Israel Info-Access is an independent publishing house committed to conveying accurate information about Israel. If your organization or service was not included, please contact us for consideration in future editions at our e-mail address:

judy@jem.ascender.com

Quantity discounts and Custom Cover orders for organizations are available through the distributor.
Tel: 1-301-897-8006.
Fax: 1-301-897-2548.

Contents

In the beginning...   3

Introduction   7

Bar and Bat Mitzvah in General   9
  Laws and Customs 9
  Traditional Shabbat Bnai Mitzvah Protocol . . .   10
  Traditional Bnai Mitzvah Practices   11
  Prayers Specific to Israel   12
  Three-Year Cycle Torah Reading   12
  Different Torah Reading in Israel   12
  Tefillin 13

It May Seem Obvious, But Ask Anyway!   15

Rent-A-Rabbi   17

Extra Special Milestones – Special Needs   21

Hassle-Free Shabbat Ceremony   25
  Jerusalem and Tel Aviv   25
  Countryside 34

Supply Your Own Rabbi and Minyan   49
  Jerusalem Locations 49
  Countryside Guest Houses in the Judean Hills . .   51

Rustic Field Schools From North to South 53

Ancient Synagogues in Safed   **59**

Ancient Synagogues in National Parks   **63**

North 64

South 66

Museum Adventures and Receptions   **67**

Weekday 3-Part Packages   **71**

Torah Tie-In Adventures   **77**

Genesis – Sefer Bereshit 78

Exodus – Sefer Shemot 92

Leviticus – Sefer Vayikra 94

Numbers – Sefer BaMidbar 95

Deuteronomy – Sefer Devarim 99

Mitzvot to Prepare at Home and Do in Israel   **103**

Theme Events   **107**

Twinning Programs   **111**

Useful Tidbits   **113**

Our Shabbat Bar Mitzvah   **118**

Web Page Sites and E-mail Addresses   **120**

Glossary   **126**

In the beginning...

We are sisters. Judy lives with her family in Israel; I live with mine in the United States. When Judy's children reached the age of Bar and Bat Mitzvah, the whole family flew over to Israel and joined their friends in marking the events. We liked the low key atmosphere of religious observance and receptions in Israel. We liked feeling connected to the land, its people, and especially, the emotionally-moving ordinariness of Bar and Bat Mitzvah celebrations. These are events that most families in Israel enjoy, not the minority of families, as in the United States.

My husband and I decided to make our son's Bar Mitzvah in Israel. To check out the feasibility and logistics of planning the event, I flew to Israel a year and a half before Josh's 13th birthday. We wanted a family Shabbat celebration in an accommodating, relaxing guest house or hotel with beautiful views and grounds, where grandparents and little children would be comfortable, and where someone else would worry about the details. After visits to a few hotels, I booked a block of rooms at Neve Ilan, a newly renovated guest house in the Judean Hills.

Remarkably, the Bar Mitzvah coincided with my husbands sabbatical from his American university. I was able to put my clients on hold, we enrolled the children in the American International School in Kfar Shmaryahu, and rented an apartment and a car for 5 months. We sent out advance notices to our entire guest list so that if they were planning a trip to Israel, they would definitely reserve that weekend to be with us. And they did! Cousins whom we had never met flew in from Australia, cousins whom we were close with flew in from London, and a college roommate and a brother scheduled their vacation time accordingly. It was not only going to be a Bar Mitzvah, it was turning into a great family reunion!

A month before the event we arranged the remaining details with the hotel and its catering staff. I ordered English language prayerbooks from a bookseller since not everyone would be comfortable with the all-Hebrew prayerbooks the hotel supplied. I then photocopied the Torah and Haftorah portion in Hebrew with English translation. We commissioned handmade pottery bowls to be placed in every guest room as a momento from the celebration. We worked on a computerized family tree which would eventually be entered into a museum data base. We bought laminated Grace After Meals booklets to be used at the meals and for guests to take home. We asked cousins to lead prayers on Shabbat and others to speak at meals. We arranged for Josh's Tefillin breakfast to mark the first time that he would wear Tefillin on the Thursday before the Bar Mitzvah. This was just an immediate family event but we did cater a small reception for the members of the morning minyan before having a Seudat Mitzvah breakfast. This was our chance for Josh to have a dress rehearsal and read the Torah in our new neighborhood synagogue. It was also a great chance to take photos. To connect Josh's Torah portion, Chayei Sarah, to the land of Israel, we reserved camels to ride in the Negev where Rebecca lowered her veil, dismounted her camel, and met Isaac. It was a whirlwind time and it was the best! To our added delight, the total bill was significantly less than a comparable time in the United States.

A few years earlier Judy's sister-in-law and family chose

to celebrate in Israel also. They spent the summer in Jerusalem and held their event on a Monday morning in the Yochanan Ben Zakai Synagogue in the Old City of Jerusalem, followed by brunch at the Laromme Hotel.

For me it was easy. My sister helped out and my husband and I had spent time in Israel previously. Back home, friends were more than curious about this adventure, they were interested in arranging one of their own. They wanted to know how to plan a Bar Mitzvah long distance – what possibilities were available, if a celebration in Israel was significantly different from an American one, how to find a Rabbi: people wanted and needed the details. So you guessed it. Judy and I had a mission all set up for us. And because most families will not have the opportunity to actually live in Israel for several months while planning the event, we wanted to present ideas that could be arranged ahead of time so that a Bnai Mitzvah celebration could be the focus of a 10-day or two week trip.

When we started to research the material for this book, we did not realize how wide the range of possibilities and original ideas would stretch. To our delight we met with creative responsible people who are excited about the Bar and Bat Mitzvah facilities and events they can offer. We gathered ideas that cover the entire country and speak to the needs of all streams of Judaism. Personally, we like the combination of Bible and the land of Israel. This is where it happened and why Israel is the perfect location to celebrate this milestone in the Jewish life of a child or adult. In Israel, G-d does not have to be added to the guest list. He is a permanent member of every minyan.

Introduction

The *Sourcebook* is for the family interested in experiencing a spiritual rite of passage and an adventure in the land of our heritage, or at least exploring alternatives to the American style Bar or Bat Mitzvah. As you are probably aware, Bar and Bat Mitzvah tours are available through various organizations. Our approach lets you avoid being locked into someone else's plans, tastes, sites and timetables. The information and suggestions we present are geared to both first-time and frequent visitors to Israel. **The *Sourcebook* will allow you to plan the entire Bar or Bat Mitzvah event by telephone, fax, or e-mail.**

Previous visitors to Israel are acquainted with the country's laid-back way of planning and doing business. While the Mediterranean business habits of the local people may be charming to a tourist, we think that anyone planning a major event needs an efficient and reliable method, indeed a professional approach. By including in the *Sourcebook* carefully chosen places and people, we present only those that meet these requirements, have excellent services to offer, and are tourist-friendly. We were selective in our choices of who and what to present. If we felt that the individuals running the business were difficult to contact, unresponsive, or unable to meet the needs of our readers, they were not included.

Our ideal Bar or Bat Mitzvah celebration consists of three parts: • the service • the reception, and • a tour or unique event that connects the land of Israel to the Torah portion that the child has mastered. We suggest ways to mix and match the possibilities listed in this book, so that the entire event reflects your interests and has a flavor unique to the land of Israel. Have the *aliyah* to the Torah on a weekday at an ancient synagogue, enjoy the festive meal – *Seudat Mitzvah* – in a setting from the time of the Mishna, and wrap it up with a Torah Tie-In Adventure.

Some families will decide to perform the ceremony itself in Israel and later throw a party back home. Others may have the actual Bar or Bat Mitzvah and party at home during the school year and then wait until the summer to conduct a symbolic ceremony in Israel. Still others will opt to have the entire celebration in Israel. The *Sourcebook* contains great ideas for all of these options. And tourists will be happy to know that the Israeli portion can be very reasonably priced – far less in fact than the average cost at home.

While we suggest ways for people from the different streams of Judaism to celebrate their Bar or Bat Mitzvah, be aware that some synagogues will permit only boys to be called to the Torah and do not celebrate Bat Mitzvahs.

All contact persons named speak English. Telephone and fax numbers are indicated for service from outside Israel. Within Israel, leave off the '972' country code, and add '0' in front of the city code.

To use this book efficiently, we suggest reading it through from cover to cover for an overview of the wonderful choices, before designing your perfect, unforgettable celebration.

The *Sourcebook* is meant to be used together with a guide book to Israel.

Bar and Bat Mitzvah in General

The celebration of Bar Mitzvah is ancient. The first Bat Mitzvah, however, is generally thought to have been in the 1920s when the daughter of Mordechai Kaplan - the founder of Reconstructionism – was called to the Torah in New York City. Conservative and Reform Jews routinely celebrate Bat Mitzvah at the age of 13 by calling the girl to the Torah. Orthodox girls also celebrate, at age 12, although generally in a different fashion. Bat Mitzvah celebrations for the Orthodox girl include *Havdallah* services, Purim-time celebrations with an all-women reading of the Book of Esther, women's *minyanim* and *Rosh Chodesh* celebrations. *Tip: Sharon Binder is an excellent resource person for creating original Bat Mitzvah event-related art work. See the Resource section for details.*

Bar or Bat Mitzvah services are held on days when the Torah is read in public – Shabbat, Monday and Thursday, holidays and *Rosh Chodesh*. On Shabbat and the first and last days of Pesach, Shavuot and Sukkot, a Haftorah is read in addition to the Torah portion.

Laws and Customs

In most established *minyanim*, some of the honors will be allotted to your family.

Note: In cases where more than eight *aliyot* are desired, some congregations break down the Torah reading into smaller portions. Check with your rabbi for exact details.

Traditional Shabbat Bnai Mitzvah Protocol

Honors

- Prayer leader for *Pesukei D'Zemra* (early morning prayers).

- Prayer leader for *Shacharit*

  Shacharit prayer leader also takes the Torah out of the Ark.

- Two *Gabbaim*. A key person in the service is the *Gabbai*, who is responsible for calling up the people for *aliyot*. He needs to know both the honoree's Hebrew name and his father's Hebrew name. It is a good idea to give the *Gabbai* a printed list of all *aliyot* together with this information. There are variations on this practice; check with your rabbi.

- Person to open the ark.

- Person to remove the Torah from the ark.

- Aliyot to the Torah:

  Aliyah 1: Cohain
  Aliyah 2: Levi
  Aliyah 3: Father, Mother, or both parents
  Aliyah 4–7: Relatives or friends
  Aliyah 8: Bar or Bat Mitzvah reads Maftir

After the child has completed his *aliyah*, the father recites a short verse relinquishing himself from responsibility for this child's sins. This may be found in the prayer book as part of the Torah service.

Note: Father and son may not follow one another consecutively in the order of *aliyot* (the *aliyah* of a father may not be followed by the *aliyah* of his son, or vice versa).

- Lift the Torah: *Hagbe*

- Dress the Torah: *Gelila*

  It is customary in some families to give the honor of sitting and holding the Torah while it is being covered to the next child in line to become a Bar Mitzvah.

- It is customary for a *Dvar Torah* (Torah commentary) to be shared at some point in the service; this may be either before the Torah reading or during the time between putting away the Torah and the *Musaf* service. It may be delivered by the Bnai Mitzvah child, a parent, the rabbi, or anyone you choose.

- The same person who opened the ark previously, returns the Torah to the ark.

- *Hazan* (cantor) for *Musaf*.

- Young child chants the closing prayers.

Traditional Bnai Mitzvah Practices

It is customary to throw candy at the Bar/Bat Mitzvah child after the Haftorah reading to symbolize sweetness and good luck. Individual pieces of candy passed around in baskets may be thrown. Some people like to throw bouquets of candy wrapped in fabric and tied with ribbon. Bring along your own materials if you are into 'do it yourself', or fax Dash Cham (see the Resource section) to prepare them for you.

Prayers Specific to Israel

During the Torah service two special prayers are added for the State of Israel which many Diaspora congregations also recite. These prayers have a special poignancy and added significance when recited within Israel.

- Prayer for the welfare of the State of Israel.
- Prayer for the welfare of soliders in the Israel Defense Forces.

Unlike in the Diaspora, where the priestly blessing is recited only on holidays, this is said every morning in Israel, and on Shabbat during the *Shacharit* and *Musaf* parts of the service. Therefore, if a Cohain is participating in the *minyan*, he should be notified of this practice in advance as he may not be acquainted with the difference in customs.

Three-Year Cycle Torah Reading

Conservative *minyanim* may or may not follow a three-year schedule. Reform congregations may follow their own schedule.

Important: If you will be joining a *minyan* for your Bar/Bat Mitzvah service, inquire ahead of time to which Torah reading schedule they adhere. Ask which Torah and Haftorah portions will be read on your Shabbat.

Different Torah Reading in Israel

During certain years the Torah portion read in Israel does not coincide with the Shabbat Torah portion in the Diaspora. In Israel the second days of Passover, Shavuot, and Sukkot are not full holidays, as in the Diaspora. If then the second day of a Festival in the Diaspora falls on a Shabbat, a special portion is read, putting congregations in the Diaspora behind a week. This is compensated for by reading double Torah portions over the following weeks. *Therefore, it is imperative that you check with a rabbi which Torah portion is to be read in Israel on the Shabbat you intend to celebrate the Bar Mitzvah. This must be done before the child begins to study the portion.*

Tefillin

> These matters that I command you today shall be upon your heart.... Bind them as a sign upon your arm and let them be ornaments between your eyes. (Deut. 6:6,8)

Many boys practice putting on their *tefillin* for several weeks in advance of their 13th birthday. During this time no blessing is recited. The first time the boy wears *tefillin* after his 13th birthday, the blessing is said, and the family may wish to attend the service. Mark this event with a *tefillin* breakfast to signify this special mitzvah. Great photo opportunity!

Tip: Hold the *tefillin* breakfast celebration on Monday or Thursday prior to the Shabbat of the Bar Mitzvah. In this way, the child can read part of his Torah portion as a sort of dress rehearsal.

Remember: The child does not get an *aliyah* on this day as that is reserved for the actual Bar Mitzvah.

The Western Wall is a meaningful place to go for this occasion. First, there is a guaranteed *minyan*. Second, you don't need to make any arrangements to pray there. Third, if the Bar Mitzvah is on a weekday, you can take memorable photographs.

Remember: If you are having a celebration on Shabbat, you may not take photographs at the Wall.

To top off the morning, have breakfast at a Jerusalem hotel.

See how *tefillin* are made.
In the Jerusalem area:
Oter Yisrael Tefillin
Tel: 972-2-653-5514
Fax: 972-2-653-5725
Address: 31 Kanfei Nesharim St.
Mercaz Sapir
Givat Shaul Industrial Area, Jerusalem 95464

For a guided tour in English, call ahead to arrange a time.

In the City of Safed, visit ex-Denverite, ex-cowboy and maker of fine saddles:

Zalmon Bear Halevy Tornek, Sofer Stam
40 Kikar HaMagenim, Safed
Tel: 972-6-692-4277
Fax: 972-6-699-9595

Purchase your son's first pair of *tefillin* here. Hear the how and why of *tefillin* and *mezuzot*. See the parchment and quills and the difference between kosher and non-kosher *mezuzot* and *tefillin*.

Call ahead to arrange a tour and talk.

It May Seem Obvious, But Ask Anyway!

Like the fourth child in the Passover story who does not know what to ask, so too are the first-time hosts of affairs in Israel. What may seem obvious to you, may very well not be so to the organizer, contact person or caterer. A general guideline is to ask questions and clarify seemingly obvious points.

RESERVING THE DATE

Reserve early, minimum one year ahead for synagogues, and avoid disappointments. Most deposits are refundable until a certain date, so it is best to book your date as soon as you can. Be sure to ask for written confirmation and a receipt for the deposit. Most synagogues and guest houses are one-of-a-kind, so if you have your heart set on a certain place, book it now! However, do not be shy to try for a date in the near future – you never know who just cancelled.

COSTS

Israel has a reputation for being an expensive country. While this is often true for those earning average salaries, there are still some good deals to be had. When it comes to renting out museums, national parks, or ancient synagogues, Israel is on the inexpensive side. Reasonable deals can be struck, and unusual and memorable events can be held.

Tip: Do not assume that certain locales are too expensive because such places would be out-of-reach in the United States. Even renting a museum after hours is not out-of-sight expensive. Check out rates and we think you will be pleasantly surprised by the range of affordable possibilities.

Tip: Ask if the rental fee for a synagogue or museum is tax deductible.

Ceremony

If you are booking a weekend at a hotel and intend to conduct a non-Orthodox ceremony, inform the hotel management. The hotel may then arrange a separate time for prayers for hotel guests who prefer an Orthodox service. If only one Sefer Torah is available, the hotel management may have to schedule one of the *minyanim* an hour earlier or later to accommodate both groups.

Food, Photos, and Music

Food. Ask if the price of the meal includes tea, wine or grape juice, soft drinks, bottled water, alcoholic drinks. Prices usually include a Bar/Bat Mitzvah cake and centerpieces.

Drinks are often served in the original bottles. If you prefer a more elegant presentation, such as pitchers, say so.

Tip: Buffet meals offer more food choices than waiter-served meals.

Photos. Point out to your photographer close family members. Ask him if his price includes negatives – it often does.

Photographer alternative: Hand out disposable cameras to all guests and collect them at the end of the event. Great collage! It is probably less expensive to bring the cameras from home.

Rent-A-Rabbi

The following people and organizations offer services to help you plan and celebrate a Bar or Bat Mitzvah in Israel. Rabbis are also a good source of information for locating musicians, photographers and caterers. If relevant, the rabbi will arrange for seating, park permits, a Sefer Torah, and prayer books.

There are many beautiful locations in the Jerusalem area to hold Bar and Bat Mitzvahs. The Haas Promenade which overlooks the Old City, the Western Wall and the Southern Wall of the Temple, and Kikar Haim on French Hill, are some of the possible sites for prayer services. If you decide to hold the service in an ancient synagogue outside of Jerusalem, the possibilities are numerous, colorful, and historically significant.

Honoraria for rabbis vary according to travel time. The rabbis listed below are based in Jerusalem. If the service is held outside Jerusalem, your contact rabbi may be prepared to travel there or may recommend a rabbi who lives closer by.

CHABAD HOUSE

CONTACT: RABBI MENDEL OSDOBA
TEL: 972-2-628-4899 (DAY)
TEL: 972-2-581-2872 (EVE)
FAX: 972-2-538-8450

Rabbi Osdoba arranges Bar Mitzvah services at the Western Wall on a Monday or Thursday morning. He can arrange for the child to be called to the Torah on Shabbat at either the Chabad synagogue in the Old City, or the Chabad synagogue in Mea Shearim. There is no charge for his services, but donations are accepted. The *minyan* is Orthodox.

JERUSALEM CONNECTION RESOURCE CENTER

CONTACT: RABBI DAVID STERN
TEL/FAX: 972-2-627-1283
ADDRESS: 3/5 HAMEKUBALIM ST., OLD CITY
JERUSALEM 97500

Jewish heritage, Hassidic, Kabbalistic outreach program. Rabbi Stern arranges Orthodox Bar Mitzvah celebrations at locations in Jerusalem and works with tour guides for locations outside of Jerusalem.

Note: Payments to Jerusalem Connection are tax deductible.

CENTER FOR CONSERVATIVE JUDAISM IN JERUSALEM

CONTACT: RABBI ED ROMM, DIRECTOR
TEL: 972-2-625-6386
FAX: 972-2-623-4127
E-MAIL: MSROMM@PLUTO.MSCC.HUJI.AC.IL
ADDRESS: 2 AGRON ST., JERUSALEM 94265

If you want a Conservative Bar or Bat Mitzvah celebration in any part of Israel, this is the place to contact. Rabbi Romm arranges the ceremony either in a Conservative synagogue or at off-beat locations around Jerusalem. He meets with the family ahead of time, and can help with photographers and music.

Note: Not all Conservative synagogues are egalitarian, and therefore the roles of women and girls may be limited

by the rules of a particular synagogue. Discuss this with
Rabbi Romm if women or girls want to participate in the
service and/or wear prayer shawls.

WORLD UNION HEADQUARTERS

CONTACT: RESERVATIONS
TEL: 972-2-620-3448
FAX: 972-2-620-3446
13 KING DAVID ST., JERUSALEM

The Reform Jewish movement – known as the Progressive Movement in Israel – is centrally located at the campus
of the World Union Headquarters in Jerusalem.

Note: Rabbi Maya Leibovitch, the first Israeli-born
woman rabbi, is willing to conduct a series of classes for
the family residing in Jerusalem for a significant period of
time prior to the Bar/Bat Mitzvah ceremony.

RABBI ROBERT BINDER

TEL: 972-2-673-1512
FAX: 972-2-671-2497
E-MAIL: BINDER@ACTCOM.CO.IL
ADDRESS: 5 HAYARDEN ST., JERUSALEM 93385

Rabbi Binder, an ordained rabbi from the Jewish The-
ological Seminary, has extensive training in the theatrical
arts. His forté is in creating imaginative Bar/Bat Mitzvah
events tied in with the relevant Torah portion.

RABBI JAY KARZEN – RITUALS UNLIMITED

RITUALS UNLIMITED
RABBI JAY KARZEN
TEL: 972-2-563-1018
FAX: 972-2-567-2068
E-MAIL: KARZEN@AQUANET.CO.IL
HTTP://WWW.ISRAELVISIT.CO.IL
ADDRESS: 1 DISKIN ST., JERUSALEM 96440

Rabbi Karzen, an Orthodox rabbi, conducts ceremonies in different styles, for affiliated and unaffiliated Jews. Rabbi Karzen sends out tape recordings of blessings and Torah readings, so the child can learn the material at home. His service is comprehensive – from ceremony, to candy throwing, to reception.

Extra Special Milestones – Special Needs

We are fortunate to have excellent opportunities in Israel for a handicapped child to celebrate the Bar/Bat Mitzvah milestone. The people and organizations listed below will take particular interest in you and your child's needs and arrange the event accordingly.

NATIONAL JEWISH COUNCIL FOR THE DISABLED

USA TEL: 212-613-8229
USA FAX: 212-613-8333
E-MAIL: NJCD@OU.ORG
ADDRESS: 333 SEVENTH AVE., NEW YORK, NY 10001

The underlying philosophy of this wonderful organization is that every child can learn something to become a Bar/Bat Mitzvah. The National Jewish Council for the Disabled, sponsored by the Orthodox Union, conducts two programs for special youth: Yachad for the Developmentally Disabled, and Our Way for the Hearing Impaired. Yachad will help arrange Bar/Bat Mitzvah preparation for Jewish youth in the U.S., from any affiliation. Although they do not work with blind people, NJCD has access to

Braille prayerbooks and Torah-reading preparation books. As a national resource center, they can often help any individual with special needs access Jewish education and/or participation in the Jewish community. Our Way can send you a *bracha* (blessings) chart to sign blessings. An NJCD representative will speak with the family rabbi and discuss preparation plans.

Tip: NJCD has contacts in Israel and can arrange for the actual ceremony to be held there.

JUDITH EDELMAN-GREEN

TEL: 972-9-767-4037
FAX: 972-9-767-9732
E-MAIL: BGREEN@POST.TAU.AC.IL

Judith Edelman-Green, National Director of the Bar/Bat Mitvah Program for the Special Child of the Conservative (Masorti) Movement, has many years of experience working with the special needs child. Her breadth of expertise and logistical know-how makes her an excellent facilitator for the family who wishes to celebrate the Bar/Bat Mitzvah milestone in Israel.

CENTER FOR THE ADVANCEMENT OF THE BLIND

P.O. Box 1132
SAFED 13111
TEL/FAX: 972-6-692-0445/6
E-MAIL: BLIND@ACTCOM.CO.IL

Bar/Bat Mitzvah ceremonies for blind or visually impaired children. The Center is based in Safed. Contact Aviva Minoff, trained to work with the blind and visually impaired, for all necessary arrangements.

AVIVA MINOFF, LICENSED TOUR GUIDE
TEL: 972-6-692-0901
FAX: 972-6-697-3116

ACHA – ASSOCIATION OF THE DEAF IN ISRAEL

CONTACT: DIRECTOR
HELEN KELLER CENTER
P.O. Box 9001
TEL AVIV 61090
TEL: 972-3-730-3355
FAX: 972-3-739-6419

Bar/Bat Mitzvah ceremonies for deaf or hearing-impaired children at the Western Wall or other significant location to suit the family.

HALLELUJAH PUBLIC RELATIONS AGENCY

CONTACT: LIMOR MANTZOURI
TEL: 972-2-652-1596; 972-52-514362
FAX: 972-2-652-6170

The expression 'heaven sent' comes to mind when I recall how we found Limor of the Hallelujah Agency. Fully aware that we needed more connections for families with special-needs children, we were checking out the relevant organizations – and getting nowhere. That same day, after a full schedule of meetings in Jerusalem, we stopped at a gas station to tank up. As I lowered my window, a man approached the car and asked for a donation to the AKIM Fund for the Mentally Handicapped. This would never have worked in the U.S., but here it felt perfectly reasonable to ask him the name of his boss. Guess who? Limor! A brilliant connection.

The Hallelujah Agency concentrates on raising funds and public awareness for handicapped people and people with special needs. Agency-owner Limor, in conjunction with an Orthodox rabbi, makes the relevant arrangements for Bar Mitzvah boys with special needs.

BAR/BAT MITZVAHS FOR ADULTS

RABBI JAY KARZEN
TEL: 972-2-563-1018
FAX: 972-2-567-2068
E-MAIL: KARZEN@AQUANET.CO.IL
HTTP://WWW.ISRAELVISIT.CO.IL
ADDRESS: 1 DISKIN ST., JERUSALEM 96440

Rabbi Karzen leads Bar and Bat Mitzvah ceremonies for adults who missed out as kids. He sends out tape recordings of blessings and Torah readings so they can learn the material at home. His service is comprehensive – from ceremony, candy throwing to luncheon. All Jews are welcome, unaffiliated or affiliated.

Hassle-Free Shabbat Ceremony

One concern families have when planning a Bar or Bat Mitzvah away from home is whether there will be a *minyan*, the necessary quorum of ten adults. Another concern is the issue of who will lead the service. This section presents options which address these concerns.

Jerusalem

The following Bnai Mitzvah locations are hassle-free on Shabbat because you join an on-going congregation, the resident rabbi and/or cantor leads the service, hotel accommodations are close by or on the premises, and the simcha can be organized by faxing just one contact person. On Shabbat, it is easiest to have all meals at your hotel. Be sure to inquire about a private dining area if you prefer to eat apart from the other hotel guests.

Note: The synagogues listed below are also available for Monday or Thursday morning services. At these times, however, you must supply the *minyan* and the rabbi or prayer leader.

Orthodox

General rules: Men and women sit separately. Married women wear a head covering. Married men wear prayer shawls. Men and boys wear *kippot*. No photography or videos on Shabbat. Women are not called to the Torah. In-house prayer books usually do not have English translation. At all synagogues, the family and Bar or Bat Mitzvah must meet with the synagogue representative at least a few days prior to the celebration.

Tip: Bring your own head covering and prayer shawl.

G REAT S YNAGOGUE

C ONTACT: E VENTS D EPT.
T EL: 972-2-624-7112
F AX: 972-2-623-3620
A DDRESS: 58 K ING G EORGE S T., J ERUSALEM 94262

- Very grand and formal synagogue.
- Handicap access.
- Escalator operates on Shabbat.

An all-male choir enhances the services on three Shabbat mornings per month.

Strictly Orthodox service. On Shabbat, the Bar Mitzvah boy is called to the Torah for an *aliyah* and the rabbi welcomes and congratulates the family. *The Bar Mitzvah boy will be allowed to read from the Torah only if the resident Torah Reader is satisfied with his fluency.*

F AMILY A FFAIRS AT THE G REAT S YNAGOGUE

On Monday and Thursday mornings, the main sanctuary of the Great Synagogue is available by prior arrangement for a family's own *minyan*. Orthodox service only.

Conveniently located in the center of Jerusalem, within walking distance of 3-, 4-, and 5-star hotels. Photo and video recording permitted on weekdays.

HEICHAL SHLOMO SYNAGOGUE

CONTACT: CATERING DEPT.
TEL: 972-50-230347
FAX: 972-2-622-3312
ADDRESS: 56 KING GEORGE ST., JERUSALEM 94262

15th-century Italian synagogue from Padua with beautiful stained glass windows. Located next door to the Great Synagogue, Heichal Shlomo has an intimate, distinctive atmosphere. Bar Mitzvahs may be held here on Shabbat with the regular congregation. Arrangements may be made for the Bar Mitzvah to read from the Torah and receive an *aliyah*.

Full service glatt kosher restaurant located in the same building. Shabbat meals and kiddush, can be arranged through the catering department. If the meals are catered at the restaurant, the synagogue rental is gratis.

FAMILY AFFAIRS AT THE HEICHAL SHLOMO SYNAGOGUE

On weekdays, Bar and Bat Mitzvah ceremonies may be held here, and photography and video recording are allowed.

Weekday meals, music, photography and receptions can be arranged by the catering department.

Conveniently located in the center of Jerusalem, within walking distance of bed and breakfast establishments, and 3-, 4-, and 5-star hotels.

CONEGLIANO VENETO SYNAGOGUE AND THE NAHON
MUSEUM OF ITALIAN JUDAICA

CONTACT: EVENTS DEPT.
TEL: 972-2-624-1610
FAX: 972-2-625-3480
ADDRESS: 27 HILLEL ST., JERUSALEM 94581

Prayer services at the Conegliano Synagogue are according to *Minhag Bnei Roma*, the Italian or Roman tradition, which has a slightly different liturgy. This tradition
is followed in synagogues in Rome and some other parts
of Italy, and in a few communities in Salonika and Con-
stantinople.

The Conegliano Veneto Synagogue and the Nahon Museum of Italian Judaica are ideal sites to celebrate the Bar
Mitzvah of a boy with family roots in Italy. The complex consists of a synagogue, museum, and reception hall
leading to a large courtyard patio. The Conegliano Veneto
Synagogue dates from 1701 and was originally located near
Venice. The synagogue was saved from destruction in the
1950s and reconstructed on its present site. The museum
displays Italian Jewish artifacts and ritual objects.

Note: The reception hall is decorated with murals of
Christian scenes painted by German missionaries. If you
don't like that motif, you can offer receptions in the courtyard, or at another location entirely.

- Sponsor a Kiddush for either the entire congregation
  or just your group in the hall or patio. Caterer rec-
  ommendations available from the staff.

- Bar Mitzvahs only.

- The rabbi or a staff member will meet with the Bar
  Mitzvah boy prior to the service so that he can practice reading from the particular Torah scroll.

- Not wheelchair accessible.

- Limited bathroom facilities.

- Maximum seating is 70 downstairs, about 20 in balcony.

- Women are seated in the balcony.

FAMILY AFFAIRS IN THE CONEGLIANO VENETO SYNAGOGUE

Bar Mitzvah ceremonies can also be held on Monday, Thursday and *Rosh Chodesh* mornings. Unlike the synagogue's Shabbat services, a private weekday service may be conducted according to the Ashkenazi or Sepharadi custom. Women and men may sit downstairs together. These are strictly family services and the family decides where men and women sit. Weekday services may include a museum tour.

Sensitive film (400 ASA) is required in the synagogue as no flash cameras or videos are permitted.

Conveniently located in the center of Jerusalem, within walking distance of bed and breakfast establishments, and 3-, 4-, and 5-star hotels.

Conservative

MORESHET YISRAEL CONSERVATIVE SYNAGOGUE

CONTACT: RABBI AVRAHAM FEDER
TEL: 972-2-625-3539
FAX: 972-2-623-4127
ADDRESS: MORESHET YISRAEL
4 AGRON ST., JERUSALEM 94265

The guidelines, standards and applications for Bar/Bat Mitzvah celebrations are available from the Moreshet Yisrael office.

Note: The Bar/Bat Mitzvah must be a student in a Jewish education program that meets the standards of the United Synagogue of America. A letter is required from the rabbi of the congregation or the Hebrew school principal confirming that these educational standards have been met. The letter and the application should be submitted with a 50% deposit.

Age is counted according to the Hebrew calendar: boys must be 13 years old plus one day; girls must have reached age 12.

Partially egalitarian.

Moreshet Yisrael is located directly in the middle of Jerusalem, within walking distance of 3-, 4-, and 5-star hotels and close to the Old City.

Reform

HEBREW UNION COLLEGE

CONTACT: RABBI SHAUL FEINBERG
TEL: 972-2-620-3305
RABBI GARY TISHKOFF
TEL: 972-2-620-3324
FAX: 972-2-625-1478
ADDRESS: 13 KING DAVID ST., JERUSALEM 94101

Alumni and families of HUC, staff, and faculty may join the congregation on Shabbat to mark their child's Bar or Bat Mitzvah.

All Bar/Bat Mitzvah families must be members of a congregation in their homeland. Bring a letter of introduction from your congregational rabbi. A list of recommended caterers is available.

Fee for ceremony includes post-service kiddush. Fees for cantor or student cantor, and accompanist, are extra. Fee for on-campus reception.

BEIT SHMUEL

For overnight accommodations, meals, and reception at Beit Shmuel:

CONTACT: CATERING DEPT.
BEIT SHMUEL YOUTH HOSTEL
TEL: 972-2-620-3470
FAX: 972-2-620-3467
ADDRESS: 13 KING DAVID ST., JERUSALEM 94101

The well maintained and beautiful campus has a youth hostel, the Skirball Archaeological Museum and the College for Academic Studies in Progressive Judaism. The entire event can be held at this centrally located facility.

The rooftop of Beit Shmuel, which is not affiliated with the Progressive Movement but rather with the Youth Hostels Association, overlooks the Old City and is a beautiful location for both service and reception. Services may be conducted on the rooftop on Monday, Thursday, *Rosh Chodesh*, Shabbat morning or Shabbat afternoon, concluding with the *Havdallah* ceremony.

The family and guests may sleep in the Beit Shmuel Youth Hostel and host a catered party on the rooftop. Sefer Torah, prayer books, prayer shawls, and *kippot* will be provided.

Note: These are family services and can be creative, with music and your own prayers. You can either prepare your own service and readings or use a more standardized text supplied by the rabbi.

HAR-EL CONGREGATION

CONTACT: BAR/BAT MITZVAH COORDINATOR
RABBI DAVID ARIEL-JOEL
TEL: 972-2-625-3841

FAX: 972-2-623-4866
E-MAIL: HARELCON@NETVISION.NET.IL
ADDRESS: 16 SHMUEL HANAGID ST., JERUSALEM
94592

Har-El Congregation welcomes Bar/Bat Mitzvah celebrations from abroad. Once initial contact has been established, Rabbi Ariel-Joel sends the child information re-
garding the relevant Torah and Haftorah portions. You
may celebrate your Bar/Bat Mitzvah at Shabbat morning
minyan, or at the Shabbat afternoon services (*mincha*).

Rabbi Ariel-Joel schedules a meeting and rehearsal with
the child and family before the celebration.

FAMILY AFFAIRS AT HAR-EL

Bar/Bat Mitzvah may choose to celebrate on a Monday
or Thursday morning at the synagogue, at Massada, or at
the Southern Wall in the Old City, or the Haas Promenade
which overlooks the walls of the Old City. Rabbi Ariel-Joel
will accompany the family to any location.

Conveniently located in the center of Jerusalem, within
walking distance of 3-, 4-, and 5-star hotels.

Tel Aviv

BEIT DANIEL

CONTACT: EVENTS DEPT.
TEL/FAX: 972-3-544-4030
ADDRESS: BEIT DANIEL, 62 BNEI DAN ST., TEL AVIV
62305

Beit Daniel welcomes Bar/Bat Mitzvah celebrations from
abroad. After a date has been set, Rabbi Meir Hazeri

sends out a tape of the relevant Torah and Haftorah readings. Prior to the celebration, Rabbi Hazeri meets with the child and family. The family joins the Shabbat morning services. Caterers available for kiddush and/or luncheon arrangements.

FAMILY AFFAIRS AT BEIT DANIEL

Bar/Bat Mitzvah may choose to celebrate on a Monday or Thursday morning at the synagogue.

Reconstructionist

CONGREGATION MEVAKSHEI DERECH

CONTACT: RABBI ARIK ASHERMAN
TEL: 972-2-679-2501
FAX: 972-2-679-6289
ADDRESS: KEHILLAT MEVAKSHEI DERECH
22 SHAI AGNON ST., JERUSALEM 92586

Families must be affiliated with a congregation or Jewish school.

Strong Reconstructionist influence.

Any boy of 13 or girl of 12 may celebrate his/her Bar/Bat Mitzvah at the congregation. At least six months before the requested date of service, the following three letters must be received by Rabbi Asherman.

- A letter from the family stating the preferred date for the service and an alternative date.

- Authorization from the rabbi or principal of a recognized Jewish religious school. The letter should indicate the extent of the child's Jewish education and participation in synagogue services. Letters from private tutors are also acceptable. In either case, the child must have at least three years of Jewish education.

- A letter from the rabbi indicating awareness of plans to hold the ceremony in Israel at this congregation.

Send or fax these letters to the attention of Rabbi Asherman at the synagogue.

Note: The family is expected to attend services at the congregation on the Shabbat prior to the event. The celebrant is expected to chant at least the Maftir from the Torah, the Haftorah and the blessings. If the child wants to chant more than this, Rabbi Asherman must be notified at least 2 months prior to the date.

A maximum of four *aliyot* will be reserved for the family.

The fee payable to the Congregation includes a non-refundable deposit to hold the date.

Overnight suggestion: Moriah Hotel, Laromme Hotel, and other hotels in that area are a 30-minute walk.

TECHILA: MOVEMENT OF SECULAR HUMANISTIC JUDAISM

CONTACT: DIRECTOR
TEL: 972-2-561-1820
FAX: 972-2-561-1359
ADDRESS: 15 ABARBANEL ST., JERUSALEM 92495

Countryside

Criteria for inclusion of guest houses or field schools in the Hassle-Free category: Almost all hotels and guest facilities in Israel are kosher and many have a synagogue on the premises. There are, however, only a handful of guest houses that are run by a religious management, from whichever stream of Judaism. These are the guest facilities we have chosen to list. A Shabbat atmosphere and special Shabbat arrangements within the affiliation you chose almost guarantees that your Bar/Bat Mitzvah celebration will be special.

Orthodox

NORTH

ALONEI HABASHAN

CONTACT: RESERVATIONS
TEL: 972-6-696-0009; 972-50-381861
FAX: 972-6-696-2503
ADDRESS: M.P. RAMAT HAGOLAN 12412

Alonei HaBashan is a religious *moshav* situated in a unique nature reserve on the Golan Heights, approximately 3 hours from Tel Aviv by car.

- Holiday bungalows: Very basic, rustic accommodations. 1 room; 2 rooms; suite (2 bedrooms + living room). All apartments have fully equipped kitchenettes.

- Glatt kosher full-service guest dining room.

Beautiful walks in the nature reserve. Guides available on the Golan Heights. Horse ranch. Trail riding. Alonei HaBashan is also an excellent place to stay overnight if the Bar Mitzvah ceremony is to be held at the ancient synagogue of Katzrin. All arrangements, including the rabbi to lead services, Sefer Torah, refreshments, transportation can be made by contacting Reservations.

MIDRESHET HAGOLAN – CHISPIN

CONTACT: RESERVATIONS
TEL: 972-6-676-3305
FAX: 972-6-676-2041
ADDRESS: M.P. RAMAT HAGOLAN 12920

- Very basic, plainly furnished 3-bedroom holiday cottages.
- Glatt kosher full-service guest dining room.
- Chispin is an excellent place to stay overnight if the Bar Mitzvah ceremony is to be held at the ancient synagogue of Katzrin. All arrangements, including the rabbi to lead services, Sefer Torah, refreshments, transportation can be made by contacting Reservations. Additional accommodations in B&B rooms at neighboring Moshav Nov.

KESHET YONATAN FIELD SCHOOL

CONTACT: RESERVATIONS
TEL: 972-6-696-2505
FAX: 972-6-696-1702
ADDRESS: M.P. RAMAT HAGOLAN 12410

The field school is located in a religious *moshav* and is part of the Keshet Yonatan Field Study Center, one of four religious field study centers in Israel. Guides explore Jewish history and biblical sources relating to the land of Israel. Moshav members welcome Bar Mitzvah families from abroad.

- Very basic, hostel-style rooms.
- Glatt kosher guest dining room.

Arrange for a guided *tiyul* (hike) on Shabbat afternoon. Field school guides are usually very knowledgeable about the geography and politics of their area.

KIBBUTZ LAVI GUEST HOUSE

CONTACT: RESERVATIONS
TEL: 972-6-679-9450
FAX: 972-6-677-9399
E-MAIL: LAVI@LAVI.CO.IL
HTTP://WWW.LAVI.CO.IL
ADDRESS: LOWER GALILEE 15267

Choice of separate synagogue for family use or participation in the guest house synagogue. For small families, you can join the kibbutz *minyan* and have some of the Torah honors.

Kibbutz Lavi runs a Bar/Bat Mitzvah Kibbutz Experience which includes pre-arrival penpal twinning with a Lavi student, tree-planting in the Lavi Forest, and a hike to the Horns of Hittin to watch the sun rise over the Golan.

- Comfortable hotel rooms.

- Glatt kosher. Special Shabbat atmosphere and arrangements.

- Conveniently located in the lower Galilee, 10 minutes from Tiberias.

MARGOA ON THE GILBOA

CONTACT: RESERVATIONS
TEL: 972-6-653-9500
FAX: 972-6-658-5895
E-MAIL: MARGOA@ACTCOM.CO.IL
ADDRESS: M.P. GILBOA 19145

Family Bar/Bat Mitzvah celebrations in an Orthodox religious kibbutz atmosphere. Participate in kibbutz synagogue services or celebrate in a private *minyan*.

- Guided Shabbat walk around the kibbutz. Hear about the geography and history of the area. See how cows are milked on Shabbat.

- Accommodations include kitchenette, private bathroom and shower in a rustic setting.

- Close to Beit Alpha National Park, Beit Shean archaeological sites.

- Guided tours and jeep trips can be arranged.

OR HAGANOZ ON HAR MERON

CONTACT: RESERVATIONS
TEL: 972-6-698-0792
FAX: 972-6-698-0795
ADDRESS: M.P. MERON HAGALIL 13909

- Glatt kosher central dining room for *moshav* members and guests.

- Very basic accommodations.

The settlement has a synagogue with a *minyan* every morning and on Shabbat. Families from abroad are welcome to pray there and celebrate their Bar Mitzvah. With advance notice, honors during the service will be allotted to the family.

NIR ETZION GUEST HOUSE

CONTACT: RESERVATIONS
TEL: 972-4-984-2542
FAX: 972-4-984-3344
ADDRESS: M.P. HOF HACARMEL 30808

- Comfortable hotel rooms.
- Glatt kosher dining room for guests.
- Guest house synagogue. Private synagogue also available.

CENTRAL

HAFETZ HAIM GUEST HOUSE

CONTACT: RESERVATIONS
TEL: 972-8-859-3776
FAX: 972-8-859-3958
E-MAIL: DAVID-V@GEZERNET.CO.IL
ADDRESS: HAFETZ HAIM GUEST HOUSE, 76817

The friendly staff at Hafetz Haim has developed an attractive Bar Mitzvah package deal. The program starts on Friday afternoon with a tractor tour of the kibbutz, a pre-Shabbat photography session of you and your family, coffee and cake. After the Friday evening meal, an Oneg Shabbat snack is served. Meals may be in a separate family dining room or with other guests. Shabbat services are in the guest house synagogue. Shabbat afternoon guided tour of the kibbutz. Gift in each room for your guests. Personalized grace-after-meals booklet. After Shabbat, a film evening and a magician entertain your party. Central location of Hafetz Haim makes this an ideal base for your stay in Israel. The reservations department can arrange a tour guide for you before or after your celebration.

- Comfortable hotel rooms.

- Glatt kosher dining room for guests.

Monday or Thursday Bar Mitzvah services also available.

SOUTH

KIBBUTZ ALUMIM GUEST HOUSE

CONTACT: RESERVATIONS
TEL: 972-7-994-9805
FAX: 972-7-994-9700
E-MAIL: ASD@SHANI.NET.IL
ADDRESS: M.P. HANEGEV 85138

Families are welcome to join the kibbutz *minyan* on Shabbat, or on Mondays and Thursdays for mid-week celebrations. Kibbutz Alumim makes sure that the honors and *aliyot* during Shabbat services go to the celebrating family.
Tip: Women may form their own *minyan* and read from the Torah to celebrate a Bat Mitzvah.

- Countryside, air-conditioned guest house facilities in a beautiful garden setting.

- Swimming pool in season. Separate swimming times for men and women.

- Kosher central dining room.

- Overnight accommodations: Air-conditioned 1- or 2-room self-contained cottages with kitchenette.

PALM BEACH HOTEL – GUSH KATIF

CONTACT: RESERVATIONS
TEL: 972-7-684-7910

FAX: 972-7-684-7215
ADDRESS: P.O. BOX 241
M.P. GUSH KATIF 79725

- Resident rabbi for Bar Mitzvah consultation.
- Glatt kosher.
- Separate men/women swimming beach and separate pool hours for weekday use.
- Located in Gush Katif.
- Comfortable hotel rooms.

Conservative

NORTH

SHALVA CONGREGATION

CONTACT: RABBI JOSEPH HECKELMAN
TEL/FAX: 972-6-692-0270
P.O. BOX 1195, SAFED 13111

- Partially egalitarian *minyan*:

    - Women are counted as part of the *minyan*.
    - Women do not receive *aliyot* to the Torah.
    - Women may read the Haftorah.

- Mixed seating.
- One-year Torah reading cycle.
- Located in the new city of Safed within walking distance of the Old City.

Suggestion: Consider hosting a reception at the Ruth-Rimon Inn in the Old City of Safed. The Inn, originally a Turkish khan, has magnificent mountain views.

MAKOM BAGALIL – MOSHAV SHORASHIM

CONTACT: RESIDENT RABBI
TEL: 972-4-990-2431
FAX: 972-4-990-2476
E-MAIL: 3784653@MCIMAIL.COM
ADDRESS: M.P. MISGAV 20164

- Resident rabbi.

- Egalitarian *minyan.*

- Prayer service is similar to an American Conservative congregation.

- Three-year Torah reading cycle. Be sure to check which is the appropriate Torah reading portion.

- Shabbat or weekday celebrations.

- Kosher central dining room.

- English-speaking members.

- Touring Programs: Tailor-made touring programs to special sites in the Galilee. Possibilities include the Mishnaic village of Zippori, neighboring Arab villages, or Safed for a family simulation game.

- Located 2 hours from Tel Aviv, 45 minutes from Haifa.

- Overnight suggestion: Family-size (room) mobile home units with bath and kitchenette.

KIBBUTZ CHANATON

CONTACT: RESERVATIONS
TEL: 972-4-986-4414
FAX: 972-4-986-4410

- Resident rabbi meets with the child and family and reviews the ceremony a few days before the actual Bar or Bat Mitzvah.

- Bar and Bat Mitzvahs.

- Kibbutz synagogue for Shabbat or daily use.

- Synagogue rental fee.

- Bed and breakfast rates. Half price for children.

- Rent-a-tour guide service available. English-speaking kibbutz members.

- Located near Nazareth

- Accommodations: Holiday cottages.

KIBBUTZ METZUBA

CONTACT: RESERVATIONS
TEL: 972-4-985-8975
FAX: 972-4-980-9337
ADDRESS: M.P. WEST GALILEE 22385

- Bar/Bat Mitzvah ceremonies may be celebrated in the Conservative or Reform style.

- Egalitarian *minyan*.

- Bar and Bat Mitzvahs.

- One-year Torah reading cycle.

- Female cantor.

- Located near Rosh HaNikra in the Western Galilee.

- Guest house on premises.

SOUTH

KIBBUTZ KETURA

CONTACT: RESERVATIONS
TEL: 972-7-635-6658
FAX: 972-7-635-6465

E-MAIL: KKOLOT@NETVISION.NET.IL
ADDRESS: M.P. EILOT 88840

- Egalitarian *minyan*.
- Bar and Bat Mitzvahs.
- Shabbat or weekday celebrations.
- Kosher.
- Shabbat observance in public places.
- English-speaking kibbutz members.
- Touring Program: The staff of Kibbutz Ketura can arrange tours of the desert tied in with relevant Jewish sources.
- Located 30 minutes north of Eilat.
- Overnight suggestion: Rustic Kibbutz Ketura accommodations or luxury hotel in Eilat.

Reform

NORTH

HAR CHALUTZ COMMUNITY SETTLEMENT

CONTACT: RABBI YAEL LAVI-ROMER
TEL: 972-4-980-3116
ADDRESS: M.P. BEEKAT BEIT HAKAREM 25129

The settlement is affiliated with the Reform Movement. Bar/Bat Mitzvah celebrations can be arranged here.

If arranged in advance, Rabbi Yael Lavi-Romer is prepared to send a tape recording of the Torah portion, meet with the family upon arrival in Israel, and then lead the service either at the Har Chalutz synagogue or at an ancient synagogue, historic setting, or alternative location of the family's choice.

Located near the town of Karmiel.
Overnight accommodations run by local families: Teva B'Har or Buki's. Use as a base for touring in the Galilee and Golan Heights.

TEVA B'HAR
HAR CHALUTZ
ADDRESS: M.P. BEEKAT HAKAREM 25129
CONTACT: HAL APPLEBAUM
TEL/FAX: 972-4-980-3666

Four Scandinavian log cabins. Each with whirlpool; kitchenette, large loft sleeping at least 3 children; master bedroom. No TV; no telephones in cabins. Minimum two-night stay. Breakfast included. Kosher.

BUKI'S
HAR CHALUTZ
M.P. BEEKAT HAKAREM 25129
CONTACT: BUKI AND ROCHELLE COHEN
TEL/FAX: 972-4-980-2471

- B&B overnight accommodations.
- Guest rooms in main house with private bathroom, cable TV, phone.
- Couples only.
- *Tip: Use for grandparents and couples who have left the little ones at home.*

KIBBUTZ MALKIYAH

CONTACT: RABBI JOHNNY MATT
TEL: 972-6-694-6815
FAX: 972-6-695-1101
E-MAIL: 100264.2724@COMPUSERVE.COM

- Resident rabbi.

- The location of Kibbutz Malkiyah gives celebrants a few choices for prayer services:

    - During the week and on Shabbat, the kibbutz synagogue, which is modeled after a 2nd century Galilean synagogue, is available.

    - Rabbi Matt can make arrangements for the use during the week of either of two nearby ancient synagogues – Baraam or Hamat Tiberias. Hamat Tiberias is an excellent choice for winter/spring celebrations, but is very hot in the summer. Baraam is located in the mountains outside of Safed – a perfect summer venue.

    - Kosher food available on request.

    - Kibbutz Malkiyah is located between Safed and Kiryat Shemona.

    - B&B overnight accommodations.

CENTRAL

KIBBUTZ GEZER

CONTACT: RESERVATIONS
TEL: 972-8-927-0646
FAX: 972-8-927-0739
E-MAIL: SEMINAR@GEZERNET.CO.IL
HTTP://WWW.GEZERNET.CO.IL/SEMINARCENTER.HTML
ADDRESS: M.P. SHIMSHON 99786

- Resident rabbi is available to meet with the Bar/Bat Mitzvah, and to lead services.

- Members practice Reform Judaism.

- Special outdoor synagogue in a park setting.

- Excellent base for touring; experience kibbutz life.

- Located 30 minutes from Jerusalem.

- Overnight suggestion: Stay at Kibbutz Gezer in very basic, hostel-style kibbutz rooms, or stay 40 minutes away at a hotel in Jerusalem and drive down to the kibbutz.

SOUTH

KIBBUTZ YAHEL

CONTACT: RESERVATIONS
TEL: 972-7-635-7968
FAX: 972-7-635-7051
ADDRESS: M.P. HEVEL EILOT 88850

- Egalitarian orientation.

- Members practice Reform Judaism.

- Bar and Bat Mitzvah celebrations.

- Kosher central dining room.

- Friendly, countryside kibbutz atmosphere.

- Guided tours of the Arava can be arranged. Hai Bar Nature Reserve is close by.

- Located 40 minutes north of Eilat.

- Overnight suggestions: Stay at the rustic country rooms of Kibbutz Yahel. Family rooms with double bed plus bunk bed, bathroom/shower facilities, kitchenette. For hotel accommodations, stay overnight in Eilat, and travel north to the kibbutz.

KIBBUTZ LOTAN

CONTACT: RESERVATIONS
TEL: 972-7-635-6935
FAX: 972-7-635-6827
ADDRESS: EDUCATIONAL TOURISM
M.P. HEVEL EILOT 88855

- Egalitarian orientation.

- Members practice Reform Judaism.

- Kosher central dining room.

- Friendly, countryside kibbutz atmosphere.

- Ask for guided tour of Timna Valley, Solomon's Pillars and rock paintings. Hai Bar Nature Reserve is close by.

- Box lunches available.

- Located 40 minutes north of Eilat at the junction of highways 90 and 40.

- Overnight suggestions: Stay at the rustic country rooms of Kibbutz Lotan. Rooms sleep up to 5 people, and have air-conditioning, bathroom/shower facilities, plus coffee corner. For hotel accommodations, stay overnight in Eilat, and travel north to the kibbutz.

Supply Your Own Rabbi and Minyan

There are many places to hold a Bar or Bat Mitzvah ritual ceremony outside of existing synagogue congregations. Your own guests will supply the quorum necessary; you can choose either to lead the service yourselves or contact a rabbi to conduct it for you.

Tip: Bring candies to throw when the child finishes reading the Haftorah.

Jerusalem Locations

YOCHANAN BEN ZAKAI SYNAGOGUE

CONTACT: ARYE
TEL: 972-2-628-0592, 02-625-4371, 02-624-8244
ADDRESS: OLD CITY, JERUSALEM

This ancient synagogue in the middle of the Old City is a photogenic and picturesque location for a weekday service. It has Mediterranean blue walls and good lighting.

- Seating downstairs for about 50 people.
- Women can sit either in the balcony or downstairs.
- No access for handicapped.
- Limited bathroom facilities.

Prayer books are all in Hebrew and follow the Sepharadi tradition but you can either bring your own or bring xeroxed sheets of the service you intend to use.

WESTERN WALL – KOTEL HAMAARAVI

HTTP://WWW.VIRTUAL.CO.IL

The Western Wall – in Hebrew, *Kotel HaMaaravi* – is an outer wall that once surrounded the Second Temple. Today it is a popular site of many Bar Mitzvah services. Advantages of celebrating a Bar Mitzvah here are the highly photogenic nature of the location, the service can be set up at the last minute, and there is never a shortage of men to make up a *minyan*. The disadvantage of celebrating at the *Kotel* is that women tend to feel left out, since the divider between the men's and women's section is high. Women are absolutely not permitted on the men's side. To circumvent this problem, hold the service near the back of the area. There is no divider there, and women can feel part of the service. In summer months, the Kotel area gets very hot by 8:30 AM. The sun is strong and there is little cloud coverage. Either finish your service before 8:30 AM or come prepared with large hats, sunglasses, and bottles of drinking water. Strict dress code enforced: head coverings for men, boys and married women. No sleeveless tops or shorts permitted.

Show up at the *Kotel* on any Monday or Thursday, or *Rosh Chodesh* morning between 6:30 and 8:30 AM.

Alternatives: Bring your own *minyan* or join a *minyan*.

GREAT SYNAGOGUE

CONTACT: BAR MITZVAH RESERVATIONS
TEL: 972-2-624-7112
FAX: 972-2-623-3620
ADDRESS: 56 KING GEORGE ST., JERUSALEM 94262

On Monday and Thursday mornings, the main sanctuary of the Great Synagogue may be opened for a family's own *minyan*, for a service in the Orthodox tradition.

Heichal Shlomo Synagogue

CONTACT: CATERING DEPT.
TEL: 972-50-230347
FAX: 972-2-622-3312
ADDRESS: 56 KING GEORGE ST., JERUSALEM 94262

During the week, Bar and Bat Mitzvah ceremonies may be held here. Photo and video recording allowed on weekdays.

Italian Synagogue and the Nahon Museum of Italian Judaica

CONTACT: RESERVATIONS
TEL: 972-2-624-1610
FAX: 972-2-625-3480
ADDRESS: 27 HILLEL ST., JERUSALEM 94581

Weekday services may be arranged, with museum tour and reception in courtyard or reception hall.
Since no flash cameras or videos are permitted in the synagogue, use sensitive film (400 ASA) for photographing.

Countryside Guest Houses in the Judean Hills

Neve Ilan Hilltop Resort

CONTACT: RESERVATIONS
TEL: 972-2-533-9339
FAX: 972-2-533-9335

E-MAIL: NEVE-ILAN@KIBBUTZ.CO.IL
HTTP://WWW.VIRTUAL.CO.IL/TRAVEL/TRAVEL/NEVEILAN
ADDRESS: M.P. HAREI YEHUDA 90850

Neve Ilan Hilltop Resort is located in the Judean Hills, about 7 miles outside of Jerusalem. This newly-renovated hotel is a great place for a family to celebrate a Shabbat Bar/Bat Mitzvah. A private synagogue with a Sefer Torah and Hebrew prayer books may be reserved. Catered meals in private dining hall may be arranged if a private room is available.

Note: Neve Ilan is the only hotel in the Judean Hills that guarantees your Bar/Bat Mitzvah Shabbat does not conflict with any other booking.

- Handicap access. Ramp. Shabbat elevator.

KIBBUTZ SHORESH GUEST HOUSE

CONTACT: RESERVATIONS
TEL: 972-2-533-8338
FAX: 972-2-534-0262
E-MAIL: SHORESH@KIBBUTZ.CO.IL
ADDRESS: KIBBUTZ SHORESH GUEST HOUSE
M.P. HAREI YEHUDA 90860

Dining with other guests in central dining room. Guest house synagogue. Special Bar Mitzvah rates.

KIBBUTZ KIRYAT ANAVIM GUEST HOUSE

CONTACT: RESERVATIONS
TEL: 972-2-534-8999
FAX: 972-2-534-8197

Lots of steps. Very hilly. Guest house synagogue.

Kibbutz Maale HaHamisha Guest House

Contact: Reservations
Tel: 972-2-533-1331
Fax: 972-2-534-2144

Guest house synagogue. Guest house dining room. Extra charge for private dining room.

Mitzpe Ramat Rahel Guest House

Contact: Reservations
Tel: 972-2-670-5555
Fax: 972-2-673-3155
E-mail: resv@ramatrachel.co.il
Address: Mitzpe Ramat Rachel
M.P. Tzfon Yehuda 90900

Dining with other guests in central dining room. Guest house synagogue.

Rustic Field Schools From North to South

The Israel Society for the Protection of Nature owns and operates a chain of rustic accommodations. These field schools are located throughout the country in areas of natural significance. A unique aspect of field schools is that they are in fact places of learning. For additional payment, a guide is available for the entire Shabbat. After Friday night dinner in the communal dining room, the guide gives a lecture about the area through which you will hike the next day.

The contact person for all field schools is Rivka Segel, as listed below. She acts as a central clearinghouse and is very well acquainted with each facility. Send a fax to Rivka, with date specifications, number of guests, and state specifically that this is a Bar/Bat Mitzvah for visitors from abroad, and all details will be dealt with.

An advantage of field schools over hotels is that they are less expensive. Accommodations are, however, very basic, and food, although plentiful, is not gourmet. Rooms sleep up to six people on bunk beds and have shower and toilet facilities.

Tip: You may prefer to put young cousins and friends together in kids' rooms and give adults their own rooms.

Below is a complete listing of the field schools by geographic area. A minimum of 30 people is needed for a Shabbat booking. Comfortable walking shoes and hats to protect from the sun are a must.

All field schools are under kashrut supervision.

CONTACT: RIVKA SEGEL
TEL: 972-3-638-8694
FAX: 972-3-688-3940
ADDRESS: SOCIETY FOR THE PROTECTION OF NATURE
4 HASHEFELA ST., TEL AVIV 61683

NORTH

HAR MERON

CONTACT: TEL AVIV HEADQUARTERS
LOCAL CONTACT: HAR MERON OFFICE
TEL: 06-698-0023, 698-9072
FAX: 06-698-7723

Specialities: Adventure hikes, rapeling, jeep trips, horseback riding, Druze hospitality.

Located on the mountainside near a Druze village.

Achziv

Contact: Tel Aviv headquarters
Local contact: Achziv office
Tel: 04-982-3762
Fax: 04-982-3015

Specialities: Jeep trips, snorkeling.
Located on a beautiful coastal strip, 6.5 km north of Naharyia.

Hof HaCarmel

Contact: Tel Aviv headquarters
Local contact: Hof HaCarmel office
Tel: 06-639-9655
Fax: 06-639-1618

Specialities: Horseback riding, boating, Druze hospitality.
Located on a beautiful coastal strip, south of Kibbutz Maagen Michael.

Keshet Yonatan

Contact: Tel Aviv headquarters
Local contact: Keshet Yonatan office
Tel: 06-696-2505
Fax: 06-696-1702

Keshet Yonatan is located in a religious settlement. Special Shabbat atmosphere and arrangements.
Specialities: Horseback riding, jeep trips, rafting on the Jordan River.
Located in the eastern section of the Golan Heights.

HERMON

CONTACT: TEL AVIV HEADQUARTERS
LOCAL CONTACT: HERMON OFFICE
TEL: 06-695-1523
FAX: 06-695-1480

Specialities: Jeep trips, horseback riding, rafting, tubing, kayaking, skiing (in season), rapeling.
Located in an oak forest.

GOLAN

CONTACT: TEL AVIV HEADQUARTERS
LOCAL CONTACT: GOLAN OFFICE
TEL: 06-696-1234
FAX: 06-696-1947

Specialities: Jeep trips, kayaking, bike trips, rapeling.
Located on the Golan Heights.

ALON TAVOR

CONTACT: TEL AVIV HEADQUARTERS
LOCAL CONTACT: ALON TAVOR OFFICE
TEL: 06-676-7798
FAX: 06-676-6770

Specialities: Jeep trips, rafting, kayaking, rapeling, horseback and donkey riding.
Located on Mount Tabor near the Kadourie Agricultural School.

JERUSALEM AREA

HAR GILO FIELD SCHOOL

CONTACT: TEL AVIV HEADQUARTERS
LOCAL CONTACT: HAR GILO OFFICE
TEL: 02-993-2386
FAX: 02-993-2644

Specialities: Desert touring, Jeep trips, donkey riding. Located near the Gilo neighborhood of Jerusalem.

SOUTH

EIN GEDI FIELD SCHOOL

CONTACT: TEL AVIV HEADQUARTERS
LOCAL CONTACT: EIN GEDI OFFICE
TEL: 07-659-4222
FAX: 07-658-4328

Attractions: Opposite the shores of the Dead Sea. Located in a nature reserve with fresh water springs and desert animals.

Located above the Ein Gedi Nature Reserve facing the Dead Sea.

SDE BOKER

CONTACT: TEL AVIV HEADQUARTERS
LOCAL CONTACT: SDE BOKER OFFICE
TEL: 07-656-5828, 656-5016
FAX: 07-656-5721

Attractions: Home and burial place of David Ben-Gurion. Solar energy project. Moonlit desert tours.

HAR HANEGEV

CONTACT: TEL AVIV HEADQUARTERS
LOCAL CONTACT: HAR HANEGEV OFFICE
TEL: 07-658-8615
FAX: 07-658-8385

Attractions: Camel and jeep tours. Rapeling. Observation terrace overlooking Ramon Crater. Bedouin hospitality tent.
Located on the rim of the Ramon Crater.

HATZEVA FIELD SCHOOL

CONTACT: TEL AVIV HEADQUARTERS
LOCAL CONTACT: HATZEVA OFFICE
TEL: 07-658-1546
FAX: 07-658-1558

Attractions: Synagogue on premises. Bedouin hospitality tent. Moonlit desert tours. Desert research station.
Located in the Arava.

EILAT FIELD SCHOOL

CONTACT: TEL AVIV HEADQUARTERS
LOCAL CONTACT: EILAT OFFICE
TEL: 07-637-1127
FAX: 07-637-1771

Attractions: Excellent snorkeling and scuba diving.
Located 7 km south of the town of Eilat. Opposite Coral Beach.

Ancient Synagogues in Safed

Safed was one of the mountaintops from which fire signals were sent to announce the New Moon and festivals during the Second Temple Period. The three picturesque Safed synagogues listed below are the ones we recommend as appropriate for Bar Mitzvah celebrations.

ARI ASHKENAZI

Named after Rabbi Isaac Luria, originally built in the 16th century. Rebuilt after an earthquake in 1837.

Vaulted ceilings, courtyard in this beautiful ancient synagogue. Orthodox *minyan* in the Ashkenazi tradition.

ABOHAV

Orthodox *minyan* in the Sephardic tradition. As we go to press, the Abohav is undergoing a facelift. Care is being taken to preserve the beautiful hand-painted murals on the ceiling, the bima, and the arks. The predominant color of the synagogue is turquoise blue. See the photograph on the *Sourcebook* cover.

KARO

Orthodox *minyan* in the Sephardic tradition. A small intimate synagogue, the Karo is named for the author of the Code of Jewish Law (*Shulkhan Aruch*), Joseph Karo, who prayed here in the 15th Century.

SAFED CONNECTIONS

• Aviva Minoff makes arrangements for a Bar/Bat Mitzvah celebrations in Safed. The ancient synagogues have an Orthodox *minyan* on Shabbat. During the week they can be reserved for family affairs. For a non-Orthodox service on Shabbat, see the Shalva Conservative congregation in the Hassle-Free section.

CONTACT: AVIVA MINOFF, LICENSED TOUR GUIDE
TEL: 972-6-692-0901
FAX: 972-6-697-3116

Suggestion: Celebrate your Bar/Bat Mitzvah on *Rosh Chodesh* in this ancient, picturesque town.
• Dror Gilboa, General Manager of Ruth-Rimon Inn, is a wealth of information. He can arrange your Bar or Bat Mitzvah celebration in any of the Safed synagogues, a reception at the Ruth-Rimon Inn, Klezmer music to liven the pace, and overnight accommodations in the hotel's luxurious rooms.

RUTH-RIMON INN HOTEL
ARTISTS' COLONY
SAFED
TEL: 972-6-692-0665
FAX: 972-6-692-0456
E-MAIL: RESERVATIONS@IRH.CO.IL
HTTP://WWW.JER1.CO.IL/TOURISM/IRH//RIMON.HTML

Safed's oldest, but newest hotel, is a splendid way to stay overnight in Safed. The Ruth-Rimon Inn was originally a Turkish khan. Happily, the hotel still has the feel of the Ottoman period, when the hotel was the postal stop along the route from Gaza to the north. Look carefully at the dining room walls and see the original tether hooks for tying up horses while the riders slept in the inn. In keeping with the original Turkish theme, the new wing sports a Turkish bath and health facility. Rooms are luxurious.

Tip: Safed is in the heart of Klezmer country – Jewish soul music. Consider Klezmer music for your bash – a sure way to liven up the party.

Tip: Instead of driving up to Safed, fly to the Rosh Pina airfield with Arkia airlines. Reserve your seat(s) on Arkia's shuttle taxi service up to Safed. Rent a car in Safed and enjoy the north. Flying time: 25 minutes from Sde Dov Airport in north Tel Aviv. Bring your passports for identification purposes.

Ancient Synagogues in National Parks

Israel has numerous ancient synagogues, attesting to the presence of Jews in Israel since time immemorial. These are certainly different, interesting and picturesque places to become a Bnai Mitzvah. Just think of the fabulous photos! Be aware though, that these are the remains of synagogues and not complete buildings.

Ancient synagogues are located in many national parks around the country. Services can be held at any of these synagogue ruins. We strongly suggest that you contact a local rabbi to make proper provisions for your Bnai Mitzvah service there. The rabbi will be your local coordinator and contact the Parks Authority for a permit, bring up a Sefer Torah and prayer books, and lead the service.

Please be aware that the park will be open to the general public when your celebration takes place. Seating may be limited and the site may be a hike from the parking lot. Extra seating can be arranged through a contact person if necessary. However, as the weekday services are usually under an hour in length, guests may not mind standing for its duration.

Whimsical tip: For that authentic feeling and some fun, populate the ancient site you chose with 'guests' from another era. Members of the Lear Theater Company, dressed in period costumes, will take active roles during the Bnai Mitzvah event.

CONTACT: LEAR THEATER COMPANY
TEL/FAX: 972-3-562-6653

North

ARBEL SYNAGOGUE

The Arbel Synagogue was built in the 4th Century and in use until the 8th Century. The site for the ark faces south toward Jerusalem. The town of Arbel dates from the time of the Maccabees.

KATZRIN SYNAGOGUE

Located in the Katzrin Talmudic Village, a reconstructed Byzantine (Talmudic) period site. Near the Golan Heights Field School. Easy access.
Overnight suggestion: Golan Heights Field School.

CONTACT: RESERVATIONS
TEL: 972-6-696-1234
FAX: 972-6-696-1947
ADDRESS: GOLAN HEIGHTS FIELD SCHOOL
KATZRIN, RAMAT HAGOLAN 12900
HTTP://WWW.GOLAN.ORG.IL/QATZRIN/TOURISTS.HTML

See Chenyon HaMapilim near Moshav Evnei Eitan (above, below) for a creative combination of prayer in an ancient synagogue with high spirited adventure.

KORAZIM SYNAGOGUE

The remains of an entire town: *Mikvah* (ritual bath) and Byzantine synagogue; oil presses, houses.

HAMAT TIBERIAS SYNAGOGUE

One of the four zodiac synagogues. Synagogue dates to the
4th Century CE. Zodaic mosaic floor. The synagogue was
destroyed in the 5th Century and rebuilt. Hamat Tiberias
is a health spa with hot springs.

Located on the western shore of Lake Kinneret (Sea of
Galilee), approximately 1.5 km south of Tiberias.

BARAAM SYNAGOGUE

Easy access – no climbing. No seats, bring your own chairs
if needed. Space for up to 2000 people!

Baraam is the site of two ancient synagogues. One synagogue dates from the 3rd Century CE. Its beauty has been
noted throughout the ages. The other is called Obadiah's
synagogue, and a part of it is in the Louvre Museum. Leg-
end has it that Queen Esther of Purim fame is buried here.
What a great place for a Purim Bat Mitzvah! Sound and
light show. Visit the website:
http://www.webscope.com/inpa/baram.html
Overnight suggestion: Har Meron Field School. 20 minutes
from Baraam.

CONTACT: RESERVATIONS
TEL: 972-6-695-1523, 694-1091
FAX: 972-6-695-1480
ADDRESS: HAR MERON FIELD SCHOOL
M.P. UPPER GALILEE

Overnight suggestion: Kibbutz Sassa vacation apartments.
10 minutes from Baraam.

CONTACT: RESERVATIONS KIBBUTZ SASSA
TEL: 972-6-698-8571
FAX: 972-6-698-8699

Overnight suggestion: Safed. 30 minutes from Baraam.
Choice of many hotels.

BEIT ALPHA NATIONAL PARK

One of the four zodiac synagogues in Israel. Well-preserved mosaic synagogue floor. Representations of zodiac signs and the Binding of Isaac. Services may be held in the ancient synagogue. Located at the foot of Mount Gilboa.

Overnight suggestions:

KIBBUTZ BEIT ALPHA GUEST ROOMS
TEL: 972-6-653-3005
FAX: 972-6-653-3611

NOF HASHITA COUNTRY LODGING
TEL: 972-6-653-6998
FAX: 972-6-653-6335
E-MAIL: INFO@GILBOA.CO.IL
HTTP://WWW.GILBOA.CO.IL

South

MAON SYNAGOGUE

The remains of this ancient synagogue date back to the Byzantine era, the 4th to 6th centuries CE. A park with water and picnic tables was built around the site – particularly useful for a celebration. An added feature of the remains is a balcony, creating an unusual seating arrangement. Located near Be'er Sheva.

ANIM SYNAGOGUE

Synagogue dating to the 4th–7th centuries. Mosaic tiles are in the outer entrance. Located in Yatir Forest.
Overnight suggestion: Stay at one of the hotels in Arad – the first Israeli town developed according to urban planning.

Museum Adventures and Receptions

Museum-based adventures are original and elegant celebrations. Contrary to your immediate possible reaction, they are not prohibitively priced. If this is a direction you find interesting, it is definitely worth pursuing. We think you will be pleasantly surprised at the affordability of the suggestions below.

TOWER OF DAVID, MUSEUM OF THE HISTORY OF JERUSALEM

CONTACT: TOURS
TEL: 972-2-627-4111
FAX 972-2-628-3418
ADDRESS: P.O. BOX 14005, JERUSALEM 91140
HTTP://JERU.HUJI.AC.IL/INFO_MUSEUM.HTML

The Museum is located in the Old City of Jerusalem near the Jaffa Gate, and is an excellent place to hold a special reception and tour. Noteworthy events featured at the Museum are the Sound and Light Show and the Murder Mystery wherein participants are challenged to solve the ancient mystery of the murder of King Herod's high priest. Special performances can be booked for a minimum of 50 guests.

HAERETZ ISRAEL MUSEUM

CONTACT: EVENTS DEPT.
2 HAIM LEVANON ST.
RAMAT AVIV, TEL AVIV
TEL: 972-3-641-5244
HTTP://EXPEDIA.MSN.COM/WG/PLACES/ISRAEL/
TELAVIV/A10440069.HTML

The HaEretz Israel Museum is located near Tel-Aviv University on beautifully landscaped grounds, the site of a Philistine city dating back to the 12th century BCE. Wheelchair accessible.

ISRAEL MUSEUM

CONTACT: EVENTS DEPT.
TEL: 972-2-670-8895/6
FAX: 972-2-563-1833
ADDRESS: P.O. BOX 71117, JERUSALEM 91710
HTTP://WWW.IMJ.ORG.IL

Curators of the Judaic department or the Youth Wing will be happy to arrange a theme tour revolving around an aspect of the child's Torah or Haftorah reading. The museum itself may be rented out during off-hours for an exclusive Bar or Bat Mitzvah event with a catered reception. Alternatively, a special event may be organized during museum hours at less expense.

BIBLE LANDS MUSEUM

CONTACT: EVENTS DEPT.
TEL: 972-2-561-1066
FAX: 972-2-563-8228
ADDRESS: 25 GRANOT ST., JERUSALEM 93706

- Fee for private 45-minute tour in any language for each group of 25 people.

- *Tip:* A few days before the tour, you choose an exhibit as the focus of the tour. Museum staff helps you choose an exhibit which ties in with the Torah portion or Haftorah the child is reading.

- *Tip:* Booklets available at front desk for self-guided treasure hunt for kids ages 7 and up.

- A festive meal can be arranged by contacting the catering department.

- Meals are catered, year round, in a covered outdoor courtyard.

- Catered meals for your private party may be held during museum hours.

- Have a private party at the museum during off-hours and arrange for tour guides. For details, contact the catering department.

CONTACT: CATERING DEPT.
TEL: 972-2-563-0058

BEIT TICHO

CONTACT: MANAGER
TEL: 972-2-624-4186
FAX: 972-2-622-3218
ADDRESS: 9 HARAV KOOK ST., JERUSALEM 94226

Beit Ticho, or Ticho House, is a branch of the Israel Museum. Located on a quiet street in the middle of Jerusalem, Ticho House is the former home of artist Anna Ticho and her noted ophthalmologist husband.

You can choose to have a reception either indoors in the art gallery or outside in the garden. Alternatively, you may rent the entire house and garden and have the museum for your guests only.

- Menu options: Dairy. Fish. Desserts.
- Photography permitted.
- Music permitted. Make your own arrangements for a band.
- No minimum number of people, but a maximum of 300.
- After-hours reception: Additional fee.

Weekday 3-Part Packages

We managed to find four places that give you the entire package: weekday prayer service, reception, and adventure based on the Bible. Each place is in a different part of the country.

NEOT KEDUMIM BIBLICAL LANDSCAPE RESERVE

CONTACT: DIRECTOR, EVENTS
TEL: 972-8-977-0777
FAX: 972-8-977-0775
E-MAIL: GEN_INFO@NEOT-KEDUMIM.ORG.IL
HTTP://WWW.NEOT-KEDUMIM.ORG.IL
ADDRESS: P.O. BOX 1007, LOD 71110

Neot Kedumim is a large nature reserve where flora and fauna found in the Bible and Talmud are grown. Also on site are ancient and reconstructed olive and wine presses.

Neot Kedumim can be the setting for the entire Bar or Bat Mitzvah. A Sefer Torah is available on the premises and the staff at Neot Kedumim is willing and able to work out a three-part celebration consisting of prayer services, a festive meal (either indoors or outdoors) with foods mentioned in the Bible, and a hands-on tour of the Reserve. Each celebration is tailor-made to suit the child's Torah or Haftorah portion.

Tip: With advance notification, your child's Torah portion can be written on parchment by a scribe.

Hands-on events include:

- Bar/Bat Mitzvah treasure hunt
- Olive harvesting (in season)
- Pita baking
- Watch a Torah scribe at work as he uses ink from nature
- Spin wool as in Biblical days
- Plant a vineyard.
- *Tip:* For an added dimension, rent biblical robes from Neot Kedumim for the celebrants.

General information:

- Handicap access.
- Reasonable prices.
- Located in the center of the country, not far from Ben Gurion airport.
- *Tip:* Golf carts are available for elderly or handicapped people so they too can take part in the tour.

CHENYON HAMAPILIM NEAR MOSHAV EVNEI EITAN

CONTACT: RESERVATIONS
TEL: 972-6-676-2151, 676-3084
FAX: 972-6-676-2044
ADDRESS: CHENYON HAMAPILIM, RAMAT HAGOLAN 12925

Located in the Golan Heights, the amenable organizers of Chenyon HaMapilim can arrange custom-made hiking/touring programs to match your family's abilities.

Range of possible activities includes:

- Donkey ride/hike through scenic El Al Canyon
- Moonlit hikes
- One hour or up to full day trips
- Return to base for kosher Israeli-style BBQ
- Sleeping arrangements in teepees or under the open sky.

Sample Bar/Bat Mitzvah program:

- Day 1: Arrive at Chenyon HaMapilim in the afternoon. Dinner arrangements in accordance with host.
- Overnight in tents.
- Day 2: Morning. Coffee and cake. Departure for the ancient synagogue in Katzrin for the Bar Mitzvah ceremony (prayer, *aliyah* to the Torah). Refreshments at the synagogue. Return to Chenyon HaMapilim for lunch.
- Afternoon. Hike through El Al Canyon.

For the entire range of possibilities, contact Menahem. He has some very good ideas for touring the Golan. Jeep and donkey tours can be arranged. Hands-on workshops on cheese- and bread-making.

Note: The site is closed on Shabbat.

Located in the north, 20 minutes from the eastern shores of Lake Kinneret (Sea of Galilee).

SOUSSIYA – RECONSTRUCTED ANCIENT TOWN

CONTACT: RESERVATIONS
TEL: 972-2-996-3424
FAX: 972-2-996-1511

Tie into history and the Jewish tradition when you visit this reconstructed Jewish town dating back to ancient times.

- Service and Torah reading by the Bar or Bat Mitzvah child on Mondays or Thursdays in the ancient synagogue of Soussiya.
- Seating is on benches.
- After the ceremony, light refreshments or a meal can be served.
- Synagogue rental fee.

Reserve an organized tour of the ancient city of Soussiya:

- Audio-visual presentation in a cave reached by going through an escape tunnel.
- Hands-on activities:
    - Restoring mosaic
    - Throwing pottery
    - Baking pita bread
    - Preparing herbal tea infusions
    - Pressing olive oil (seasonal)
    - Riding on donkey
    - Pressing grapes for making wine (seasonal).

Tip: Make arrangements to watch a Torah scribe at work.
Located in the Hebron Hills.
Overnight suggestion: Hostel on site. Double rooms and family rooms – all with private shower/bathroom.

KFAR KEDEM MISHNAIC VILLAGE

CONTACT: EVENTS DIRECTOR
TEL: 972-6-656-5511
FAX: 972-6-656-9759
ADDRESS: KFAR KEDEM
MITZPE HOSHAAYA
M.P. NAZARETH ILLIT 17915

Kfar Kedem is a reconstructed village from the time of the Mishna. Guests are outfitted in clothing suitable for village life 500 years ago in the Galilee and ride donkeys to get around. Feast on traditional foods in a shepherd's tent.

Experience life as a shepherd in an ancient town in the Galilee:

- Grind wheat and bake bread

- Make your own mosaic

- Press olive oil

- Stamp grapes for wine-making

Suggestions:

- Celebrate the Bar Mitzvah with an *aliyah* to the Torah at the Orthodox synagogue of Mitzpe Hoshaaya (5 minutes from Kfar Kedem).

- Celebrate the Bar or Bat Mitzvah with an *aliyah* to the Torah at the egalitarian Conservative *minyan* at nearby Kibbutz Chanaton.

- After morning services at either location, continue to Kfar Kedem for a day of adventure.

Overnight suggestions:

KIBBUTZ CHANATON
TEL: 972-4-986-4414
FAX: 972-4-986-4410

ZIPPORI VILLAGE
TEL: 972-6-646-2647
FAX: 972-6-646-4749
E-MAIL: PILCER@RANNET.COM

Zippori Village on Moshav Tzipori. Four air-conditioned/heated guest cabins, beautifully decorated with handmade mosaic tiles, Jacuzzi, loft sleeping area, fully-equipped kitchenette. Kosher breakfast delivered to your cabin.

- All arrangements can be made through the Events Dept. of Kfar Kedem.
- Located in the north, near Zippori National Park.

Torah Tie-In Adventures

Two places pertinent to any Torah portion are the Bible Lands Museum in Jerusalem and Neot Kedumim Biblical Landscape Reserve near Ben Shemen. These sites can be included as part of a Bar/Bat Mitzvah adventure or just visited on their own.

The Bible Lands Museum is arranged by biblical eras and its galleries include, for example, The Age of the Patriarchs and When Israel Sojourned in Egypt. Each exhibit is highlighted by relevant Torah verses. Bnai Mitzvah tours focus on the requested Torah or Haftorah portion. See the section on Museum Receptions for details about arranging tours and receptions in the museum.

Neot Kedumim is a 650-acre biblical landscape reserve close to Ben Gurion airport. Bnai Mitzvah may be either specific to the celebrant's Torah or Haftorah reading or be on a topic of general biblical interest, such as The Shepherd as Leader. See Weekday 3-Part Packages for details.

Torah Tie-In Adventures links specific biblical verses, events and personalities to special Bnai Mitzvah adventures in Israel. This unique, and admittedly less than scholarly approach, should be considered with a smile. However, we firmly believe that any and all of these adventures will enrich the entire celebration. Obviously, feel free to do adventure tours from anywhere in the list; don't be limited to the portion your child is reading.

Genesis – Sefer Bereshit

TREES

> God said: Let the earth bring forth vegetation,
> herbs yielding seed, fruit trees yielding fruit ...
> and so it was. (Gen. 1:11)

Plant a tree at a Jewish National Fund center. Daily except
Shabbat. Each planter receives a certificate, a lapel pin and
the tree planter's prayer. Cost per tree: $10. Ask about
special Bar/Bat Mitzvah group plantings. See Theme section for invitations to a tree theme event.

JEWISH NATIONAL FUND TREE PLANTING
TEL: 177-022-3484 (TOLL-FREE IN ISRAEL)
TEL: 1-800-542-8733 (TOLL-FREE IN THE USA)

Tree planting centers are located around the country.

- Jerusalem area: Hadassah Forest and the Kiryat Mena-
  hem Forest.
- Modiin area (center of the country): Ben Shemen
  Forest. Buses leave from 96 HaYarkon Street, Tel
  Aviv. Wheelchair accessible.
- North: Lavi Forest at the Golani Junction
- South: Birdwatching Center in Eilat. Eilat is part
  of the migratory route for birds flying between Asia
  and Africa.

Alternatively, plant a grapevine at Neot Kedumim. The
'Kerem (vineyard) Mitzvah' program allows you to help
restore barren land to green fertility. The planting area
is located next to a Talmudic-era winepress, and ancient
terraces, enabling visitors to clear stones from the fields, as
in ancient times. Visitors may irrigate their newly planted

grapevines with water from an ancient cistern and then rest on a roofed, mosaic-floor winepress while imbibing the fruit of the vine.

CONTACT: DIRECTOR, EVENTS
TEL: 972-8-977-0777
FAX: 972-8-977-0775
E-MAIL: GEN_INFO@NEOT-KEDUMIM.ORG.IL
HTTP://WWW.NEOT-KEDUMIM.ORG.IL
ADDRESS: P.O. BOX 1007, LOD 71110

LIVING CREATURES

> On the fifth day, God said: "Let the waters teem with living creatures, and fowl that fly ... and on the sixth day, God said: "Let the earth bring forth living creatures, each according to its own kind." (Gen. 1:20,25)

God created animals. Adam named them. Noah saved them. Animals were a sign of wealth. Animals got you to and fro. Animals plowed the fields. Animals were indispensable!

JERUSALEM

Whimsical tip: The Tisch Biblical Zoo in the Manhat neighborhood of Jerusalem has an excellent interactive computer display at the entrance to the zoo. The animated program, with Noah as host, features a zoo tour in the footsteps of animals featured in the Bible; the animals are referenced according to source.

TISCH BIBLICAL ZOO
TEL: 972-2-643-0111
FAX: 972-2-643-0122
ADDRESS: P.O. BOX 898
MANHAT, JERUSALEM 91008

SOUTH

Hai Bar Yotvata. 40 minutes north of Eilat. Be sure to take part in the night tour to see nocturnal animals in action. Phone for English tour schedule.

HAI BAR YOTVATA
VISITOR CENTER
TEL: 972-7-637-6018

Timna Valley Park is located 16 miles north of Eilat. Majestic sandstone mountains can be climbed. Egyptians mined copper here as early as the third millennium. Ancient rock drawings of wild animals can be seen at the Chariot's Site.

TIMNA VALLEY PARK
VISITOR CENTER
TEL/FAX: 972-7-635-6215

Snorkeling and diving with dolphins. Be sure to call ahead for reservations.

DOLPHIN REEF IN EILAT
TEL: 972-7-637-5935
FAX: 972-7-637-5921

Rent snorkeling gear at Coral Beach and swim with the fish. Visit the underwater observatory.

CORAL BEACH OBSERVATORY IN EILAT
TEL: 972-7-637-6929
FAX: 972-7-637-5776

Ride alpacas and llamas in the desert.

ALPACA AND LLAMA FARM IN THE NEGEV
TEL: 972-7-658-8047
FAX: 972-7-658-6104

Whimsical tip: All Bar/Bat Mitzvah celebrants can wear t-shirts of Noah and the ark, available at the Bible Lands Museum store in Jerusalem.

RAINBOWS

> I have set My rainbow in the cloud, and it shall be a sign of the covenant between Me and the earth. (Gen. 9:13)

In Hebrew the word for rainbow and arc are the same: *keshet.* Hike to Me'arat Keshet (Arc or Rainbow Cave) – a cave without a roof, now an arc-like suspension bridge. Fabulous view. Northern part of the country.

BREAKING BREAD

> Avraham hurried to the tent and said to Sarah, "Hurry, three measures of meal, fine flour! Knead and make cakes!" (Gen. 18:6)

Avraham welcomed his guests in the tent by offering them freshly baked bread. As it turns out, his guests were angels.

Drink coffee or tea, or eat a full meal as you experience typical Middle Eastern hospitality in a Bedouin tent.

MAMSHIT CAMEL RANCH
TEL: 972-7-655-1054; 972-7-655-4012
FAX: 972-7-655-0965
HTTP://WWW.RAMAT-
NEGEV.ORG.IL/TOUR/MAMSHIT.HTML

2.5 miles east of Dimona. Sleeping and eating in Bedouin
tent. Kosher. Camel trips.

ANGEL'S BAKERY
GIVAT SHAUL INDUSTRIAL AREA
JERUSALEM

Whimsical tour: For an off-beat escapade, visit the popular
Angel's Bakery in the Givat Shaul section of Jerusalem.
The bakery is open 24 hours a day, closed from Friday
afternoon until after Shabbat. Join the singles crowd and
visit the bakery for hot muffins in the middle of the night.

Jerusalem at Night: Visit any challah bakery on Thursday night close to midnight in the Mea Shearim neighborhood. The aroma alone is worth the trek.

CAMELS

> And the servant [Eliezer] took ten camels of his
> master's camels and departed ... (Gen. 24:10)

Energy-efficient camels were a sign of wealth in days of
yore. Take the group camel-riding and experience this ancient and reliable transportation system.

SOUTH

MAMSHIT CAMEL RANCH
SEE ABOVE.

TZEL MIDBAR – DESERT SHADE
TEL: 972-3-575-6885
FAX: 972-3-613-0161

Adventures in the Ramon Crater, the Negev, the Spice Trail Jeep and Camel Tours. Professionally run. For information on this general area, see the Negev Highlands website: http://www.ramat-negev.org.il.

CAMEL RIDERS DESERT EXPLORATION TOURS
TEL: 972-7-637-3218
FAX: 972-7-637-1944

Jeep tours, bike tours, special interest tours in 'Genesis' country. Day or week-long camel trips.

DEAD SEA

> All the kings came as allies...to the Salt Sea.
> (Gen. 14:3)

Swim in the salty Dead Sea. If you prefer to stay dry, cross over the Jordanian border on a 'Lot's Wife' Dead Sea cruise. Meals can be arranged on board if ordered in advance.

LOT'S WIFE DEAD SEA CRUISE
TEL: 972-7-659-4760
FAX: 972-7-658-4137

DONKEYS

> So Abraham woke up early in the morning and
> saddled his donkey... (Gen. 22:3)

Kfar Kedem is a reconstructed village from the time of the Mishna. Hands-on activities. Menahem can arrange for morning services and *aliyah* to the Torah at the Orthodox synagogue of Mitzpe Hoshaaya. He can also arrange for an egalitarian or Conservative morning service and and/or overnight accommodations at nearby Kibbutz Chanaton.

DONKEY TRAILS
TEL: 972-6-656-5511
FAX: 972-6-656-9759
ADDRESS: MITZPE HOSHAAYA
M.P. NAZARETH ILLIT 17915

Tie into history and the Jewish tradition when you visit this reconstructed Jewish town dating back to ancient times.

SOUSSIYA
RESERVATIONS
TEL: 972-2-996-3424
FAX: 972-2-996-1511

For more information on Soussiya, see Ancient Synagogues in Nature.

CHENYON HaMAPILIM NEAR MOSHAV EVNEI EITAN
RESERVATIONS
TEL: 972-6-676-2151, 676-3084
FAX: 972-6-676-2044

See the section, Weekday Adventures.

HEAVENLY STARS

> ...In multiplying I will multiply thy seed as the
> stars of the heaven... (Gen. 22:17)

Count the stars of the heaven when you take a night time desert jeep tour. Get out of the jeep, lie down on the ground and start counting.

TZEL MIDBAR – DESERT SHADE
TEL: 972-3-575-6885
FAX: 972-3-613-0161

Adventures in the Ramon Crater, the Negev, the Spice Trail Jeep and Camel Tours.

JEEPERS DESERT JEEP TOURS
TEL: 972-7-997-1235
FAX: 972-7-997-1423

Custom jeep tours, mainly in the south.

NEGOTIATING

When purchasing the burial grounds for Sarah, Abraham said about Ephron the seller:

> ...he may give me the cave of the Machpelah, which he has, which is in the end of his field; for the full price let him give it to me... (Gen. 23:9)

Abraham didn't bargain over the cave's price. But you can enjoy bargaining in fine Mid-Eastern tradition. Go to the shuk, the market place in Jerusalem's Old City and bargain over everything – a response the merchants expect.

COINS

> And [Abraham] weighed for Ephron the silver...
> four hundred shekels of silver... (Gen. 23:16)

Weights rather than coins were used in Biblical days. See examples of shekels and other ancient weights, coins and seals.

ERETZ ISRAEL NUMISMATIC PAVILION
2 HAIM LEVANON ST.
RAMAT AVIV, TEL AVIV
TEL: 972-3-641-5244

Tip: If the Bar/Bat Mitzvah celebrant is a coin collector, a great gift is a special issue Israeli coin commemorating the occasion. The coins are minted in different weights of gold and silver.

ISRAEL GOVERNMENT COINS & MEDALS CORP. LTD.
IN JERUSALEM:
5 AHAD HAAM ST.
TEL: 972-2-560-0100
FAX: 972-2-561-2298
IN TEL AVIV:
3 MENDELE ST. (NEAR THE DAN HOTEL)
TEL: 972-3-522-7428

NABATEANS

> These are the names of the sons of Ishmael...the
> first born of Ishmael, Nebaiot... (Gen. 25:13)

The descendants of Nebaiot were known as the Nabateans. Visit the Nabatean cities of Avdat, Mamshit and Shivta. Avdat is a National Park site which includes a small museum and video show. Shivta has a reconstructed working Byzantine farm using ancient farming methods.
Culinary experience: Dushara Nabatean Restaurant is on a hilltop in the ancient city of Mamshit. Magnificent views. Restaurant decor and tableware convey the feeling of the lost civilization of the Nabateans. Exotic foods are spiced with local spices and herbs. Highly recommended. Kosher. Closed on Shabbat. Reservations suggested.

DUSHARA NABATEAN RESTAURANT
MAMSHIT NATIONAL PARK (NEAR DIMONA)
TEL: 972-7-655-5743
HTTP://WWW.RAMAT-
NEGEV.ORG.IL/TOUR/MAMSHIT.HTML

ARCHERY – BOWS AND ARROWS

> Now therefore take, I pray thee, thy weapons,
> thy quiver and thy bow, and go out to the field,
> and take me venison... (Gen. 27:3)

And what can be more genuine than to shoot bows and arrows in a biblical landscape? Experience the excitement of desert archery in the wondrous natural desert setting of Mizpe Ramon.

DESERT ARCHERY PARK
TEL/FAX: 972-7-658-7274
ADDRESS: P.O. BOX 581, MIZPE RAMON 80655
HTTP://WWW.ISRAELVISIT.CO.IL/DESERT.HTML

WELLS

> Isaac's servants came and told him about the
> well they had dug and said we have found wa-
> ter. And he called it Sheva. Therefore the name
> of the city is Be'er Sheva until this day. (Gen.
> 26:32,33)

Water was scarce and wells were critical. Wells were also a meeting place (the first town center). All the Patriarchs dug them. Be'er Sheva National Park has archaeological ruins over 6000 years old. Among them is the well identified as the very one where Abraham and Isaac made a peace pact with the Philistines, and from where the city got its name, Be'er (well) Sheva (oath). A large and complex water system was uncovered within the park. Worth a visit.

BE'ER SHEVA NATIONAL PARK
TEL: 972-7-646-7286

Whimsical tour: Mey Eden Water Factory on the Golan Heights. Israelis today drink water from this major supplier of fresh mineral water. Tours of the production plant are given for a fee. Check for times of English language tours.

MEY EDEN VISITORS CENTER
TEL: 972-6-696-1050
ADDRESS: KATZRIN INDUSTRIAL AREA
HTTP://WWW.MEYEDEN.CO.IL

Whimsical tour: Take a tour of the national water carrier in the northern part of the country at Sapir Site. Water from Lake Kinneret (Sea of Galilee) is carried to all parts of the country *via* the carrier.
Note: The tour must be reserved at least two weeks in advance by faxing the names and passport numbers of participants and the desired tour date. Bring all passports to the tour itself. Be sure to request the English language video and tour. Tour length: Approximately one hour.

SAPIR SITE PUBLIC RELATIONS DEPT.
TEL: 972-6-671-4770
FAX: 972-6-672-6399

MATRIARCHS AND PATRIARCHS

> God said, "Take your son, your only one, whom you love and go to the land of Moriah." (Gen. 22:2)

Binding of Isaac: Tradition has it that the *Akedah* (binding) took place on what later became the Temple Mount – and the site of the Holy of Holies. Today the Mosque of Omar stands on this site. However, excavations under the Western Wall bring us to a spot just opposite the Holy of

Holies. Take a tour of the excavations below the Temple Mount.

TOUR: ATERET HACOHANIM OLD CITY TOURS
TEL: 972-2-589-5101
HTTP://WWW.VIRTUAL.CO.IL/ORGS/ORGS/ATERET

TOUR: ARCHAEOLOGICAL SEMINARS
TEL: 972-2-627-3515
FAX: 972-2-627-2660
E-MAIL: STERN-I@ARCHESEM.CO.IL
ADDRESS: P.O. BOX 14002, JERUSALEM 91140

Mosaic floors of two ancient synagogues portray the binding of Isaac:

BEIT ALPHA NATIONAL PARK
LOCATED ON KIBBUTZ HEFTZIBA
TEL: 972-6-653-2004

Perfect location for the Bnai Mitzvah party too!

ZIPPORI NATIONAL PARK
TEL: 972-6-656-8272
HTTP://WWW.WEBSCOPE.COM/INPA/ZIPPORI.HTML

> And Isaac brought [Rebecca] into the tent of
> Sarah his mother, he married Rebecca and she
> became his wife.... (Gen. 24:67)

Sleep in a tent in the desert like Rebecca and Isaac did.

MAMSHIT CAMEL RANCH
TEL: 972-7-655-4012
HTTP://WWW.RAMAT-
NEGEV.ORG.IL/TOUR/MAMSHIT.HTML

Day trip desert experience, including a Beduin meal, available every Friday.

CONTACT:
UNITED TOURS
TEL: 972-3-522-2008
HTTP://WWW.INTOURNET.CO.IL/UNITEDTOURS/
TOUR185.HTML

> And Avraham buried Sarah his wife in the cave
> of the field of Machpelah which is Hebron. (Gen.
> 23:19); Avraham died and his sons Isaac and
> Ishmael buried him in the cave of Machpelah.
> (Gen. 25:8-9)

Tour the ancient city of Hebron where Abraham and Sarah are buried. Check with your hotel for times of guided tours.

JEWISH COMMUNITY OF HEBRON
HTTP://WWW.VIRTUAL.CO.IL/COMMUNITIES/
ISRAEL/HEBRON

SHEPHERDS AND FLOCKS

> And Jacob said: ...I will pass through all of
> your flock today, removing every speckled and
> spotted goat, and every dark one among the
> sheep... and that shall be my pay. (Gen. 30:31,32)

Go to Neot Kedumim and take the tour: The Shepherd as Leader. Sheep and goats were important to all Biblical figures.

> And the angel said: Your name shall not be
> called Jacob, but Israel, for you have striven
> with God and with men and you have prevailed."
> (Gen. 32:29)

Jacob wrestled with the angel and was given the new name 'Israel'.

Conduct a service, complete with food and tour at the Palmach Cave where the State of Israel got *its* beginning. Call ahead to arrange tour and a Zionist experience.

PALMACH CAVE
ON KIBBUTZ MISHMAR HAEMEQ
TEL: 972-4-989-6847

Or combine your stay in Tel Aviv with a visit to Independence Hall where David Ben-Gurion signed the Proclamation of Independence. Continue to Ben-Gurion's home in Tel Aviv, now a free-entry museum.

INDEPENDENCE HALL
16 ROTHSCHILD BLVD., TEL AVIV
TEL: 972-3-517-3941
HOURS: SUNDAY – THURSDAY: 9 AM –2 PM

HOME OF DAVID BEN-GURION
17 BEN-GURION BLVD., TEL AVIV
TEL: 972-3-522-1010
HOURS: SUNDAY, TUESDAY–THURSDAY: 8 AM–3 PM;
MONDAY: 8 AM–5 PM; FRIDAY: 8 AM–1 PM

Audio-visual show at Ben-Gurion's country retreat, on the grounds of Kibbutz Sde Boker, in the southern part of the country. Call for information.
COUNTRY RETREAT OF BEN-GURION
KIBBUTZ SDE BOKER
TEL: 972-7-656-0320
SOUND AND LIGHT SHOW
KIBBUTZ SDE BOKER
TEL: 972-7-656-5717

Exodus – Sefer Shemot

The Ten Plagues

> And God said to Moses: "Stretch out your hand
> toward heaven, that there may be darkness over
> the land of Egypt, even darkness which can be
> felt." (Ex. 10:21)

While we cannot – and prefer not to – experience all ten
plagues, we can feel what total darkness was like. Prepare
yourselves with candles when you visit the Flour Cave near
Sodom by the Dead Sea. Arrange with your tour guide.

Or experience the opposite and learn about Solar Research in the Desert. Call ahead to reserve a tour.

Solar Research Center at Midreshet Sde
Boker
Sde Boker Field School
Tel: 972-7-655-5059
Fax: 972-7-655-5060

The best way to sense the exodus itself is to go to the
desert. Have an adventure tour with any of the tour guides.
If you can get to Mt. Sinai, terrific! A few days in any part
of the desert should give you the idea.

Altars

> For if you make Me an altar of stone, do not
> build it of hewn stones; for if you lift your tool
> on it, you have profaned it. (Ex. 20:22)

An example of the altar described in the portion of Jethro
is found at Tel Arad.

Tel Arad National Park
Near the town of Arad

OIL AS FUEL

> And thou shalt command the children of Israel,
> that they bring unto thee pure olive oil beaten
> for the light, to cause a lamp to burn continu-
> ally. (Ex. 27:20)

Explore the olive oil storage caves at Bet Guvrin and Tel
Maresha. Besides the storage caves, complete dwellings
have been unearthed here. Catered parties can be arranged
near the caves. This is tricky business – Rabbi Binder and
other resource people excel in putting together such an
affair.

BET GUVRIN NATIONAL PARK
TEL: 972-7-681-1020
FAX: 972-7-681-2957

PRIESTLY GARMENTS

> And you shall make holy garments for Aaron
> your brother, for splendor and for beauty ...a
> breastplate, and an ephod, and a robe and a
> tunic of chequer work, a mitre....(Ex. 28:1,4)

The laws concerning the priestly garments, the breastplate,
the crown, and the brass laver, the incense and perfumes,
the special blue color used to dye holy garments, and the
shewbreads are complex. These ritual items have been
recreated and are on display in the Old City of Jerusalem.

TREASURES OF THE TEMPLE
19 MISGAV LADACH ST.
JEWISH QUARTER
OLD CITY, JERUSALEM
TEL: 972-2-626-4545

Reservations suggested for English language tour and
video show.

SPICES OF THE TEMPLE

> Take the finest spices, of flowing myrrh. . .and of
> sweet cinnamon. . . and of sweet calamus. . .and
> of cassia. . .and of olive oil. . ..And make it a holy
> anointing oil. . .and anoint the meeting tent and
> the ark of the covenant. (Ex. 30:23-38)

Reuven Prager of Beged Ivri, a commercial enterprise, re-
searches and restores ancient Israelite customs. Among the
products offered is a set of Ketoret – spices of the Temple.

BEGED IVRI
111 AGRIPPAS ST.
JERUSALEM
TEL: 972-2-625-8943
HTTP://WWW.ISRAELVISIT.CO.IL

Leviticus – Sefer Vayikra

PRIESTLY SPICES

> And you will put oil on it, and lay frankincense
> on it; it is a meal offering. (Lev. 2:15)

Take an amazing tour of the Nabatean Spice Trail. The
Nabateans were nomads who traveled the impenetrable
desert selling spices. The trail began in Petra and ended in
Gaza. Along the way the Nabateans found and hid water
sources. They traveled with 1000 camels laden with spices.
Eventually they built way stations, two of which you can
see. One is Mamshit and the other is Avdat. Contact a
desert tour agency listed in Resources for details on a camel
or jeep tour of the Spice Trail. If it's not possible to take
an extensive tour, at least tour these ancient cities.

Mamshit National Park
Tel: 972-7-655-6478

Avdat National Park
Tel: 972-7-655-0954

Culinary experience: Dushara Nabatean Restaurant (in the park) is on a hilltop in the ancient city of Mamshit. Magnificent views. Restaurant decor and tableware convey the feeling of the lost civilization of the Nabateans. Exotic foods are spiced with local spices and herbs. Highly recommended.

Dushara Nabatean Restaurant
Tel: 972-7-655-5743
http://www.ramat-negev.org.il/tour/mamshit.html

Kosher. Closed on Shabbat. Reservations suggested.

Numbers – Sefer BaMidbar

Signs of the Zodiac

The arrangement of the Twelve Tribes around the Tabernacle as they marched through the desert relates to the signs of the zodiac! Go to an ancient synagogue and see the zodiac mosaics. See Theme Events. Celebrate in one of the zodiac synagogues.

Beit Alpha National Park
Located on Kibbutz Heftziba
Tel: 972-6-653-2004

Zippori National Park
Tel: 972-6-656-8272
http://www.webscope.com/inpa/zippori.html

NAZARITES

> "A man or woman who shall disassociate him-
> self by taking a Nazarite vow of abstinence for
> the sake of God shall abstain from new or aged
> wine and he shall not drink vinegar of wine or
> vinegar of aged wine; anything in which grapes
> have been steeped he shall not drink, and fresh
> and dried grapes he shall not eat." (Num. 6:2)

Nazarites were not permitted to drink wine or eat grapes.
Visit a winery to see what they were missing!

GOLAN HEIGHTS WINERY VISITORS CENTER
KATZRIN INDUSTRIAL CENTER
TEL: 972-6-696-2001, 972-6-696-1646
HTTP://WWW.GOLANWINES.CO.IL/GW2.HTML

Golan Heights Winery produces Yarden, Gamla, and Golan
labels. Call at least one week in advance for tour. Be sure
to request English-speaking guide.

AMIAD WINERY
TEL: 972-6-693-3869

Wines and liquors are made also from fruits other than grapes: pear, kiwi, raspberry, kumquat – to name but a few. Tour and tasting. English tour times are on the hour. Closed Shabbat and Jewish holidays.

CARMEL MIZRACHI WINERY
TEL: 972-3-964-2021
25 HACARMEL STREET
RISHON LEZION

Call for English tour hours.

CARMEL MIZRACHI WINERY
TEL: 972-6-639-0105
WINE STREET
ZICHRON YAAKOV

Call ahead to arrange tour.

PRIESTS – COHANIM

> God spoke to Moses, saying, "Speak to Aaron and his sons, saying: So shall you bless the Children of Israel saying to them: 'May God bless you and keep you. May God illuminate His countenance for you and be gracious to you. May God lift His countenance to you and establish peace for you.' " (Num. 6:22-26)

Today the role of the Cohanim is limited to blessing the congregation during the daily morning services in Israel, and on holydays in the Diaspora. In the time of the Temple, the role of the Priest was much more extensive and vital to the spiritual life of the Jewish people.

TREASURES OF THE TEMPLE
19 MISGAV LADACH ST.
JEWISH QUARTER
OLD CITY, JERUSALEM
TEL: 972-2-626-4545

WOHL ARCHAEOLOGICAL MUSEUM JEWISH QUARTER
OLD CITY, JERUSALEM
TEL: 972-2-628-3448

Reservations suggested for English-language tour and video show.

DESERT ROUTES

> And the Canaanite, the king of Arad, who dwelt
> in the South, heard tell that Israel came by the
> way of the Atarim, and he fought against Israel
> and took some of them captive. (Num. 21:1)

Derech HaAtarim is the route between the Negev and the Sinai. It went through Be'er Sheva, Machtesh Ramon and part of the Sinai Desert. Arrange with your tour guide.

> The she-donkey saw the angel of God and crouched
> beneath Balaam. Balaam's anger flared and he
> struck the she-donkey with the staff. (Num.
> 22:27)

Adventure: See Adventures in the Book of Genesis.

Deuteronomy – Sefer Devarim

TRAVELS IN THE WILDERNESS

> So we passed by our brethren the children of
> Esau, that dwell in Seir, by way of the Arava,
> from Eilat and from Etzion-Geber. (Deut. 2:8)

Travel the route from South of the Dead Sea to the Gulf of
Eilat. The Israelites wandered in the Arava, King David
captured it from the Edomites and King Solomon built a
harbor and copper mines there.

RIVER JORDAN

> God said to Moses, "Ascend to the top of the
> cliff and raise your eyes westward, northward,
> southward, and eastward, and see with your
> own eyes, for you shall not cross the Jordan."
> (Deut. 3:27)

The Jordan River: The entry to the Promised Land. But
neither Moses nor Aaron made it to the other side. Now
you are here! At the same river. Raft, kayak and swim.

KAYAK KFAR BLUM
TEL: 972-6-694-8755; 690-2616
KFAR BLUM
M.P. UPPER GALILEE 12150

DESERT AFFLICTIONS

> You shall remember the entire road on which
> God led you these forty years in the Wilderness
> so as to afflict you.... (Deut. 8:2)

After 40 years of wandering in the desert, the mothers and big sisters definitely needed pampering: facials and relaxing massages are currently available at hotels along the Dead Sea. Choose any Dead Sea resort and soak it up! Highly recommended.

Note: If the fathers and big brothers need some tender loving care, they too can check this out.

COPPER MINES

> Moses describes Israel as a land where "...the stones are iron, and out of whose hills you may dig brass."

Do not miss Timna Park, the ancient and magnificent mining area 40 minutes north of Eilat.

THE TEN COMMANDMENTS

> Moses called all of Israel and said to them: "Hear O Israel, the decrees and the ordinances that I speak in your ears today; learn them, and be careful to perform them." (Deut. 5:1)

Moses conveyed the Ten Commandments to the Jewish people. On a more judicious note, visit the new Supreme Court in Jerusalem.

SUPREME COURT
NEAR THE KNESSET
JERUSALEM
TEL: 972-2-675-9612

Call for tour times in English.

WATER, WATER EVERYWHERE...

> Israel is a land of streams of water, of springs
> and underground water coming forth in valley
> and mountain. (Deut. 8:7)

Swim in the spring of Ein Gedi near the Dead Sea.

Climb, swim, dive, jump in the Yehudiyya Canyon in
the Golan Heights.

Mitzvot to Prepare at Home and Do in Israel

Ziv Tzedakah Fund, Inc.
A non-profit tax exempt corporation
Danny Siegel, Chairman
Contact in the U.S.:
Naomi Eisenberger
USA Tel: 973-763-9396
USA Fax: 973-275-0346
E-mail: naomike@aol.com
Contact in Israel:
Arnie Draiman
Israel Tel: 02-671-5945

Many families see the occasion of celebrating Bar/Bat Mitzvah as an opportunity to emphasize the importance of the individual role we each have in 'Tikun Olam' – putting the world aright. The celebrant him or herself is usually eager to actively participate in Tikun Olam as a way of making an immediate contribution to the Jewish community and humanity at large. Parents are often interested in teaching their child that the newly conferred status of 'adult' brings with it the responsibility of positive contribution.

We have chosen a very special *tzedkah* (charity) fund in Israel which will give teenagers the chance to be active participants in *tzedekah*.

The Ziv Tzedakah Fund carefully screens its recipients and distributes supplies to a wide variety of people in Israel. They include special needs children and adults, elderly people, victims of terrorism, blind people, abused and battered women, and desperately poor people.

Listed below are items needed for distribution in Israel. If you want to bring the donation yourself, you may get a chance to help serve a meal at a shelter or soup kitchen or play wheelchair basketball against some tough players. But if your schedule doesn't allow that, just arrange for a drop off time. Either way, be sure to let the Ziv Tzedakah Fund know that you're collecting and bringing the items. Then be sure to arrange a meeting time to drop off or bring the packages to their recipients.

The Bar/Bat Mitzvah child can either buy these items or collect them from classmates, neighbors, relatives, etc. One boy put a basket in the synagogue lobby asking for toothbrushes for a Free Dental Clinic in Jerusalem. Dentists who were members of the synagogue contributed their free samples and Hebrew School students each brought in a couple. After two months, he had collected over 400 toothbrushes and toothpaste tubes. He then brought them to the Clinic during his trip to Israel. It was an important and much appreciated contribution.

Please contact the Fund before beginning to collect the items and let them know what you're doing. (Also, tell them you read this book). If you have other ideas besides those listed below, discuss them with the the Fund's American or Israeli representatives. For example, if you know someone who owns a factory or store and has goods to give away which are not specially listed below, find out if the Tzedakah Fund has a use for them. If you would rather collect Tzedakah money and buy food in Israel to give to a food shelter, that's fine too.

ITEMS NEEDED IN JERUSALEM FOR DISTRIBUTION BY ZIV TZEDAKAH FUND, INC.

Clothing: New or used but in good condition. Clothing for adults, children and babies. Jeans, sweaters, socks, stockings, jackets, gloves and hats, baseball caps, tee shirts, etc. Towels and washcloths are also needed. Clothing is bulky and unless you're willing to bring an extra suitcase, its probably impractical to collect clothing and towels to give away. However, if you are coming to Israel with a group of people, you can collect everyone's used tee-shirts or beach towels, for example, and donate them at the end of the trip.

Dental supplies: Toothbrushes, toothpaste, floss, any dental tools.

Games and toys: Cards, coloring books, crayons and markers, glue sticks, paint sets, stuffed animals, dolls, blocks, small sporting equipment like balls or jump ropes. English language books are not needed.

Hearing aids: Behind the ear hearing aids are needed. Don't bring the type of hearing aid that goes into the ear itself as those have to be fitted.

Medical leftovers: Operating rooms often have extras from sterile kits such as suture threads, rubber gloves, sponges, gauze, tape, etc. Even if the items are no longer sterile, they can be used for purposes other than medical.

Over the counter medical supplies: Aspirins, cold medicines, thermometers, band-aids, allergy medicines, creams and ointments, etc.

Pet food: This may be too heavy to carry on your trip. You may decide to buy pet food in Israel and bring it with you when visiting the animal shelter.

Sewing supplies: Spools of thread, fabric, velcro, zippers, snaps, scissors.

Toiletries: Toiletries must be new. Small samples are good as are regular size items; hotel or airline samples are a perfect contribution. Some things which are particularly expensive in Israel but not in the U.S. are sunscreen, moisturizers, deodorants, mouthwash. Other ideas are combs and brushes, makeup, barettes for girls' hair, nail clippers.

Wedding dresses and veils: Be on the lookout for wedding gowns of relatives or close friends. Put an announcement in your synagogue's news bulletin requesting gowns for donation. Gowns are bulky and difficult to pack; even one or two dresses is a useful contribution.

Theme Events

ECOLOGY AND ENVIRONMENTAL AWARENESS

Create a theme and contribute to a worthwhile cause by buying Bar/Bat Mitzvah invitations, place cards, and thank you notes from the Jewish National Fund. JNF plants trees with the proceeds – kind of like recycling – trees → paper → new trees. A $500 order plants a Garden of Trees in Israel – the child receives a laminated plaque and his/her name appears in the Book of Gardens. Be sure to plant a tree yourself.

CONTACT: JNF IN THE USA
1-800-542-8733

TOGA PARTY

CARDO CULINARIA RESTAURANT
TEL: 972-2-626-4155
FAX: 972-2-628-4238
ADDRESS: P.O. BOX 14002
JERUSALEM 91400
HTTP://WWW.INTOURNET.CO.IL/ARCHSEM/CARDO.HTML

In a category all by itself – literally – the Cardo Culinaria is more than a restaurant: it is an event. Located in the Jewish section of the Old City of Jerusalem, the Cardo Culinaria presents authentic Roman meals. To add to the atmosphere, guests are given Roman togas to wear and period music is played.

Open daily except Shabbat from noon to 2 PM. Evenings by reservation only.

Location is excellent for a reception after services in the Yochanan Ben Zakai Synagogue.

ROOTS!

BETH HATEFUTSOTH – MUSEUM OF THE JEWISH
DIASPORA
SEMINAR DEPT.
TEL: 972-3-646-2020
FAX: 972-3-646-2134
ADDRESS: P.O. BOX 39359
TEL AVIV 61392
HTTP://WWW.BH.ORG.IL/INDEX.HTML

For a family wishing to add an extra dimension to the Bar/Bat Mitzvah journey to Israel, digging up family roots can be rewarding. The Dorot (Hebrew for 'generations') Project of the Museum of the Jewish Diaspora is a computerized family tree database. All data come from families and individuals who enter their personal geneologies into the computer. Either prepare your family history in writing and pay the Dorot staff to enter the material, or enter the data on a disc which will be uploaded into the Museum's database at no charge. Be sure to ask Dorot staff which computer program to use. Check the website for on-line information on data entry. http://www.bh.org.il/Geneology/index.html.

A private seminar discussion and tour can be set up for a minimum of ten people. This seminar would focus on the general paths and directions that Jews took throughout the centuries and not on the specifics of any particular family. For example, if an ancestor lived in Florence and the family ultimately wound up in the United States, the seminar will show the general path people took in those years and show models of synagogues and photos of towns where Jews lived. The Seminar Department has age-appropriate activities for the different family members participating in the seminar.

SIGNS OF THE ZODIAC AND JEWISH EQUIVALENTS

The relative position of the constellations in the sky corresponds to the positions of the tribes around the ark in their travels in the Wilderness.

Tip: Salvador Dali designed a series of coins based on the Twelve Tribes for the Israel Government Coins & Medals.

ISRAEL GOVERNMENT COINS & MEDALS CORP. LTD.
5 AHAD HA'AM ST., JERUSALEM
TEL: 972-2-560-0100
FAX: 972-2-561-2298

ZODAIC SIGNS

We have paired up corresponding Zodiac signs with each of the appropriate Twelve Tribes, the Hebrew month, and the holiday during that period.

- Aries the Ram – Judah – Nissan – Passover
- Taurus the Bull – Issachar – Iyar – Independence Day
- Gemini the Twins – Zebulun – Sivan – Shavuot
- Cancer the Crab – Reuben – Tammuz
- Leo the Lion – Simeon – Av – Fast of Ninth of Av
- Virgo the Virgin – Gad – Elul – Time of repentance

- Libra the Balance – Ephraim – Tishre – New Year; Yom Kippur
- Scorpio the Scorpion – Manesseh – Cheshvan
- Sagittaurus the Archer – Benjamin – Kislev – Chanukah and the month of rainbows
- Capricorn the Goat – Dan – Tevet
- Aquarius the Water Bearer – Asher – Shevat – Tu B'Shevat - New Year of the Trees
- Pisces the Fish – Naftali – Adar – Purim

Twinning Programs

JEWISH HOLOCAUST SURVIVORS

Jewish Holocaust Survivors and Friends of Greater Washington sponsor a twinning program with Yad Vashem, the Holocaust Memorial Museum in Jerusalem. A Bar or Bat Mitzvah child may 'twin' with a child who died in the Holocaust. A Scroll of Remembrance is sent to the celebrant. Donations are accepted but not required and may be given either to the Holocaust Museum in Washington, DC, or to Yad Vashem in Jerusalem. Contact the program chairman, Samuel Speigel, at least two months in advance.

REMEMBER-A-CHILD
USA TEL: 301-593-4562
10607 Woodsdale Avenue
Silver Spring, MD 20901

AMIT – ISRAEL'S OFFICIAL NETWORK FOR RELIGIOUS AND TECHNOLOGICAL EDUCATION

AMIT sponsors a twinning program. For $200 the Bar/Bat Mitzvah child receives a certificate, medal and letter stating the name of a child with a similar birthdate in one of the AMIT-sponsored schools. Correspondence between the two children is encouraged.

AMIT FUNDRAISING DEPT.
USA TEL: 212-477-4720
USA FAX: 212-353-2312
E-MAIL: AMITCHLDRN@AOL.COM

KIBBUTZ LAVI

Part of the Bar/Bat Mitzvah Kibbutz Experience run by
Kibbutz Lavi in the Galilee is a twinning pen pal program.
Prior to arriving in Israel, and after having made arrangements to celebrate the occasion on Kibbutz Lavi, the child
is teamed up with a Kibbutz Lavi child for correspondence.
Eventually the two children will get together on the kibbutz.

RESERVATIONS
TEL: 972-6-679-9450
FAX: 972-6-677-9399
E-MAIL: LAVI@LAVI.CO.IL
HTTP://WWW.LAVI.CO.IL
ADDRESS: KIBBUTZ HOTEL LAVI
LOWER GALILEE 15267

Useful Tidbits

Ministry of Tourism

Tel: 972-2-675-4877
Fax: 972-2-675-4974
Address: 57 King George St., Jerusalem 94262

Bar/Bat Mitzvah participants receive a certificate and gift from the Ministry of Tourism. Write to the Ministry at least two months in advance. Include the child's English name, Hebrew name, father's name, and date and location of service. Call the Ministry a week before the celebration to arrange for pick-up of the gift.

Note: A boy receives a *tallit* (prayer shawl) which he can wear to his Bar Mitzvah ceremony. If an Israeli rabbi is helping with the service, the rabbi will contact the Ministry for you.

Anglo Israel

Contact: Joan Summerfield
Tel/Fax: 972-9-771-0588
E-mail: anglo@netvision.net.il
http://www.feldcom.com/anglo

Joan has excellent contacts and many years of experience in putting together a memorable simcha in Israel. Coordinates entire event.

BAR/BAT MITZVAH RITUALS

HTTP://WWW.BIBLE.ORT.ORG

"Navigating the Bible", produced by the World ORT Union, is an information-packed Web sight for information about Bar/Bat Mitzvah rituals and history. Plug in a birth date to find out the Torah and Haftorah portions read on your Bar or Bat Mitzvah, both in Israel and in the United States. *Remember:* Torah readings in Israel may differ from those in the U.S.

DASH CHAM UNIQUE BASKETS AND GIFTS

TEL: 972-2-672-2355; 2-672-4673
FAX: 972-2-672-4673
ADDRESS: TALPIOT MALL, JERUSALEM
E-MAIL: JBASKETS@VIRTUAL.CO.IL
HTTP://WWW.VIRTUAL.CO.IL/VJ/ADVERTISING/DASH

The owners of Dash Cham will prepare wrapped candy for throwing at the Bar/Bat Mitzvah, hostess gifts, centerpieces, and welcome gifts to put in the hotel rooms of your guests. It is not necessary to go to the store – all arrangements, including delivery, can be handled by phone.

DAVID BELLIN TRAVEL SYSTEMS

TEL: 972-4-997-6241
FAX: 972-4-997-2242
E-MAIL: DBELLIN@ACTCOM.CO.IL
HTTP://WWW.TALI.COM/ISRAEL

All Bnai Mitzvah arrangements including service, reception, tour.

FLY-A-CAKE

IN THE US, 1-800-419-9951.
IN ISRAEL, 02-533-6704

Beautiful, original, delicious cakes in just about any shape
or form. See their cake catalog for possibilities.

HOUSE OF HARRARI

TEL/FAX: 972-2-625-5191
E-MAIL: HARRARI@VIRTUAL.CO.IL
HTTP://WWW.VIRTUAL.CO.IL/ART/HARRARI
ADDRESS: 7 NACHLAT SHIVA ST., JERUSALEM

Hand-made harps created from beautiful woods, just like
King David once played.

IN STYLE EVENTS LTD.

CONTACT: ESTEE AND EDNA
TEL/FAX: 972-3-643-1704
44/28 TAGORE ST.
TEL AVIV 69341

From A to Z arrangements. A hassle-free event.

INTOURNET VIRTUAL TRAVEL AGENCY

HTTP://WWW.INTOURNET.CO.IL

Reservations for hotel, car, etc. on-line.

KESHET EDUCATIONAL TOURISM

TEL: 972-2-561-2045
FAX: 972-2-563-7497
E-MAIL: YSOKO@NETVISION.NET.IL
ADDRESS: P.O. BOX 1065, EFRAT 90435
U.S. TRAVEL OFFICE: 1-800-826-9485

Keshet is an independent, pluralistic and professional in-
stitution devoted to educational travel in Israel. Yitzhak
Sokoloff, Director, customizes family and group tours to
meet the disparate needs of children and adults. Keshet
specializes in both teenage and family programs that combine the spiritual and physical beauty of Israel, and offers
the possibility of integrating a Bnai Mitzvah experience
into a private or group tour that is off-the-beaten track.

MABAT TOURING SERVICES

TEL: 972-3-961-8930
FAX: 972-3-961-8940
E-MAIL: MABATOUR@INTER.NET.IL
HTTP://WWW.MEMBERS.TRIPOD.COM/MABAT

Years of experience in creating and delivering special and
unique Bnai Mitzvah events. All arrangements including
service, reception, tour.

SAFED CANDLES

TEL: 972-6-692-1093
FAX: 972-6-692-2557
ADDRESS: P.O. BOX 377, ARTISTS' COLONY, SAFED

Beautiful pure beeswax hand-made candles for Shabbat,
Havdallah, Chanukah, and just plain ambience. Workshop
on premises. Worth a visit.

SHARON BINDER ART WORKS

TEL: 972-2-673-1512
FAX: 972-2-671-2497
ADDRESS: HAYARDEN 5, JERUSALEM 93385
E-MAIL: BINDER@ACTCOM.CO.IL

Well-known Jerusalem-based artist adds a personal touch to your celebration. Commission Sharon to draw your family tree, design your invitations and matching souvenir prayer service booklet. Consider a personalized, illuminated *Book of Esther* or *Book of Ruth* to mark your daughter's Bat Mitzvah. Personalized, appliquéd *tallit* and *tefillin* bags made to order. Commissioned works have been presented to the Prime Minister of Israel, the late Yitzhak Rabin, and to His Majesty King Hussein of Jordan. Book early!

Our Shabbat Bar Mitzvah

WELCOME TO JOSH'S BAR MITZVAH CELEBRATION
PARSHAT CHAYEI SARA
NEVE ILAN, HAREI YEHUDA

The computer-generated Family Tree which is hanging downstairs is for you to add to and perhaps correct. As the family gathers, this is the perfect opportunity to get to know
our common ancestry. The program will be entered into
the Beth Hatefutsoth – Museum of the Jewish Diaspora's
geneology database.

In your rooms you will find pottery bowls, hand-made
by Michal, for you to keep as a memento of Josh's Bar
Mitzvah.

Friday

- Photograph session with Josh and the rest of us:
  2:00–4:00 PM
- Coffee and Cake: 3:00–4:15 PM
- Shabbat candlelighting in the main lobby: 4:08 PM
- Mincha and Kabbalat Shabbat led by Grandpa
  Hector: 4:23 PM
- Dinner: 6:30 PM

Shabbat

- Coffee and Cake: 7:30–8:30 AM
- Shacharit led by Edward: 8:30 AM
- Torah service led by Eitan and Jay
- Torah and Haftorah readings by Josh
- Musaf led by Joel
- Priestly Blessing led by Ronald
- Kiddush: 11:00 AM

- Lunch: 12:00 noon
- Dvar Torah by Josh
- Mincha led by Edward: After lunch
- Hike led by Joel: After Mincha
- Seudat Shlishit (third meal): 4:15 PM
- Maariv and Havdallah to mark the end of Shabbat: 5:30 PM

Post-Shabbat

- Drive to Jerusalem with our guests from Melbourne, London, and New York.
- Early Sunday morning departure for camel trip in the Negev. Experience the desert as described in Josh's Torah portion, Chayei Sarah. This is where Rebecca lowered her veil, dismounted her camel, and met Isaac.

The snack bar in the main lobby is open for your use throughout Shabbat. Let the server know you are from the Rosenbloom party.

Shabbat Shalom
Deborah, David, Josh, Lila

Web Page Sites and E-mail Addresses

ANGLO ISRAEL

- E-mail: anglo@netvision.net.il
- http://www.feldcom.com/anglo

ARCHAEOLOGICAL SEMINARS

- E-mail: stern-i@archesem.co.il
- http://www.intournet.co.il/archsem

ATERET COHANIM

- http://www.virtual.co.il/orgs/orgs/ateret

BARAAM

- http://www.webscope.com/inpa/baram.html

B&B COUNTRY LODGING IN ISRAEL

- http://www.tour-israel.co.il

BEGED IVRI

- http://www.israelvisit.co.il

BETH HATEFUTSOTH – MUSEUM OF THE JEWISH DI-ASPORA

- http://www.bh.org.il/index.html

CARDO CULINARIA RESTAURANT

- http://www.intournet.co.il/archsem/cardo.html

CENTER FOR THE ADVANCEMENT OF THE BLIND

- E-mail: blind@actcom.co.il

DASH CHAM GIFTS & BASKETS

- E-mail:JBaskets@virtual.co.il
- http://www.virtual.co.il/vj/advertising/DASH

DAVID BELLIN TRAVEL SYSTEMS

- E-mail: dbellin@actcom.co.il
- http://www.tali.com/israel

DESERT ARCHERY PARK

- http://www.israelvisit.co.il/desert.html

DUSHARA NABATEAN RESTAURANT

- http://www.ramat-negev.org.il/tour/mamshit.html

GOLAN HEIGHTS WINERY

- http://www.golanwines.co.il/gw2.html

HAFETZ HAIM GUEST HOUSE

- E-mail: david-v@gezernet.co.il

HAR EL CONGREGATION

- E-mail: harelcon@netvision.net.il

HAERETZ ISRAEL MUSEUM

- http://expedia.msn.com/wg/places/
  Israel/TelAviv/A10440069.html

HOUSE OF HARRARI

- E-mail: harrari@virtual.co.il
- http://www.virtual.co.il/art/harrari

INTOURNET VIRTUAL TRAVEL AGENCY

- http://www.intournet.co.il

ISRAEL HOTEL ASSOCIATION

- http://www.virtual.co.il
- E-mail: infotel@israelhotels.org.il

ISRAEL INFO-ACCESS

- E-mail: judy@jem.ascender.com
- E-mail: torbloom@erols.com

ISRAEL MUSEUM

- http://www.imj.org.il

JEWISH COMMUNITY OF HEBRON

- http://www.virtual.co.il/communities/israel/hebron

JUDITH EDELMAN-GREEN

- E-mail: bgreen@post.tau.ac.il

KATZRIN ANCIENT SYNAGOGUE

- http://www.golan.org.il/qatzrin/tourists.html

KESHET EDUCATIONAL TOURISM

- E-mail: ysoko@netvision.net.il

KIBBUTZ ALUMIM GUEST HOUSE

- E-mail: avidwor@ibm.net

KIBBUTZ ALUMIM GUEST HOUSE

- E-mail: avidwor@ibm.net

KIBBUTZ GEZER

- http://www.gezernet.co.il/seminarcenter.html

KIBBUTZ KETURA

- E-mail: kkolot@netvision.net.il

KIBBUTZ LAVI GUEST HOUSE

- http://www.lavi.co.il
- E-mail: lavi@lavi.co.il

KIBBUTZ SHORESH GUEST HOUSE

- http://www.virtual.co.il
- E-mail: shoresh@kibbutz.co.il

KIDS JERUSALEM ADVENTURES

- http://www.intournet.co.il/kids
- E-mail: kidsjlmadv@netmedia.co.il

MABAT TOURING SERVICES

- http://www.members.tripod.com/mabat
- E-mail: mabatour@inter.net.il

MAKOM BAGALIL – MOSHAV SHORASHIM

- E-mail: 3784653@mcimail.com

MAMSHIT CAMEL RANCH

- http://www.ramat-negev.org.il/tour/mamshit.html

MAPS OF ISRAEL

- http://www.hotelstravel.com/israel.html#mp

MARGOA ON THE GILBOA

- E-mail: margoa@atcom.co.il

MASORTI (CONSERVATIVE) CONGREGATIONS IN ISRAEL

- http://www.virtual.co.il/masorti/masorti

MEY EDEN MINERAL WATER PLANT

- http://www.meyeden.co.il

MITZPE RAMAT RACHEL GUEST HOUSE

- http://www.virtual.co.il
- E-mail: resv@ramatrachel.co.il

MUSIC FACTORY

- http://www.cyberscribe.com.il
- E-mail: perkins@netmedia.net.il

NATURE RESERVES AUTHORITY

- http://www.nature.co.il

NEGEV HIGHLANDS

- http://www.ramat-negev.org.il

NEOT KEDUMIM BIBLICAL LANDSCAPE RESERVE

- http://www.neot-kedumim.org.il
- E-mail: gen_info@neot-kedumim.org.il

NEVE ILAN GUEST HOUSE

- http://www.virtual.co.il/travel/travel/neveilan
- E-mail: neve-ilan@kibbutz.co.il

NOF HASHITA COUNTRY LODGING

- http://www.gilboa.co.il
- E-mail: info@gilboa.co.il

ORTHODOX UNION

- http://bible.ort.org/bible/html
- E-mail: njcd@ou.org

RABBI ROBERT BINDER

- E-mail: binder@actcom.co.il

RABBI JAY KARZEN – RITUALS UNLIMITED

- http://www.israelvisit.co.il
- E-mail: karzen@aquanet.co.il

RABBI ED ROMM

- E-mail: msromm@pluto.mscc.huji.ac.il

RABBINICAL ASSEMBLY OF ISRAEL

- E-mail: raisrael@jtsa.edu

RUTH-RIMON INN

- http://www.jer1.co.il/tourism/irh//rimon.html

SHARON BINDER ART WORKS

- E-mail: binder@actcom.co.il

TOWER OF DAVID MUSEUM

- http://jeru.huji.ac.il/info_museum.html

UNITED TOURS

- E-mail: unitedtours@intournet.co.il
- http://www.intournet.co.il/unitedtours

WESTERN WALL

- http://www.virtual.co.il

WORLD ORT UNION

- http://bible.ort.org/bible/html

ZIPPORI NATIONAL PARK

- http://www.webscope.com/inpa/zippori.html

Glossary

ALIYAH TO TORAH Saying a blessing before an individual
Torah reading and after the reading. Before reciting
the blessings, the fringes of the tallit are touched on
the name of God and then kissed. The word 'aliyah'
means to 'go up to', 'ascend'. There are eight *aliyot*
during a Shabbat or holiday Torah reading. The first
aliyah is reserved for a descendent of a Cohain, or
priestly tribe. The second *aliyah* is reserved for a
Levi, or descendent of the tribe of Levi. The rest of
the *aliyot* are given to family and friends. The last
aliyah is reserved for the Bar/Bat Mitzvah child. Traditionally, a father and son do not have consecutive
aliyot.

ALIYOT Plural of Aliyah.

ASHKENAZI Person or tradition stemming from Jews from
Germany, Russia, Poland, Hungary.

BNAI MITZVAH Girls celebrate Bat Mitzvah, boys celebrate Bar Mitzvah and collectively they are all Bnai
Mitzvah.

HAZAN Person who chants the prayers in front of the congregation.

COHAIN Descendent of the priestly tribe. Usually identified by a last name such as Cohen, Kahn, Kahane,
etc.

DVAR TORAH Literally, words of Torah. A short talk dis-
cussing the Torah portion of the week. A Dvar Torah
can be given by the Bnai Mitzvah child before or after
the Torah service or at one of the celebration meals.

GABBAIM Two people who stand on either side of the
Torah as it is being read. One of them calls up the
individuals for the Aliyot and also recites their names

in blessings after the Aliyah. The second one is there to help find the place in the scroll, if needed, and just as an additional helper.

GELILA Lifting the Torah after it is read. This individual should be strong and able to lift an unrolled scroll high up and then sit down with it intact.

HAGBE The person who binds the Torah and dresses it with its sash, cover, and crowns.

HAVDALLAH The ceremony marking the close of the Sabbath and Holidays. A multi-braided candle, sweet smelling spices and a glass of wine or grape juice are used to usher out the Sabbath and welcome the new week.

KIBBUTZ A collective society on which many families live. Kibbutzim often have guest houses for guests who want to experience communal life.

KIDDUSH The prayers sanctifying the wine during the Sabbath and holidays.

KLEZMER Jewish soul music.

KOSHER Ritually pure food which may be eaten by a Jew. There are many different degrees of kosher. Do not assume all food sold in Israel is kosher. Certificate of Kashrut is granted to eating establishments that meet kashrut guidelines.

LEVI Descendent of the tribe of Levi. See ALIYAH.

MINYAN Quorum of ten adults, i.e., above Bar Mitzvah age. Men required to form a prayer group. In some non-orthodox congregations, a minyan may include adult women, i.e., above Bat Mitzvah age. A minyan is required if the Torah is going to be read in public.

MOSHAV Type of collective settlement in Israel. On a moshav, families live in their own houses and eat their meals at home. They share ownership of heavy equipment needed for farming and pool their agricultural resources.

MUSAF Additional prayers recited on Shabbat and Holidays only.

PESUKAI D'ZIMRAH Early morning prayers.

ROSH CHODESH The new moon. The Jewish calendar is lunar and the sighting of the new moon is celebrated every month. The Torah is read on Rosh Chodesh even when the latter falls on a weekday. If Rosh Chodesh coincides with Shabbat, an additional Torah portion is read. Rosh Chodesh is either one or two days, depending on the month.

SEPHARDI A person or tradition stemming from Jews from Spain, Portugal, Morocco, the Arab lands, Bulgaria, Romania, Latin America.

SEUDAT MITZVAH A festive meal celebrating the performance of certain mitzvot (commandments), such as becoming Bnai Mitzvah, a marriage, a circumcision.

SHACHARIT Morning prayer service.

SIDDUR Prayer book.

TALLIT Prayer shawl.

TEFFILIN Phylacteries traditionally worn during weekday morning services by Jewish men over the age of 13.

TIYUL Hike.